The Authors

Derek Dykes

For twenty years, from 1983 to 2003, Dykes was one of Scotland's most-formidable casuals. A founder member of the Hibs Capital City Service he helped organise some of the bloodiest encounters in the annals of football hooliganism. For his trouble he racked up more than fifty convictions for violence and also enjoyed two spells at Her Majesty's pleasure in Barlinnie prison. He was a contributor to the Sky Television documentary series *The Real Football Factories*. Dykes has now given up football violence and is a contented family man. He lives in Edinburgh with his partner and their three children.

Andy Colvin

Sun journalist Colvin has expert knowledge of the casual scene. In the 1980s, at considerable personal risk, he went underground to infiltrate Aberdeen's notorious mob, the ASC, in order to write the definitive account of the phenomenon for his former newspaper, the *Sunday Post*. He also appeared in *The Real Football Factories*. Colvin lives in central Scotland with his wife.

These Colours Don't Run: Inside the Hibs Capital City Service

Derek Dykes and Andy Colvin

FORT PUBLISHING LTD

First published in 2007 by Fort Publishing Ltd, Old Belmont House,
12 Robsland Avenue, Ayr, KA7 2RW

Printed by Bell and Bain Ltd, Glasgow

Cover art by Andy Bridge

Graphic design by Mark Blackadder
Typeset by Senga Fairgrieve

Thanks to the *Edinburgh Evening News* for permission to reproduce the
article on pp 157–9.

ISBN: 978-1-905769-07-0

Derek Dykes

Andy Colvin

CONTENTS

PREFACE

Take a stroll through the Scottish Football museum at Hampden Park and you'll come across the usual collection of jerseys, medals and memorabilia. Move into the popular-culture section and there are turnstiles, old sections of terracing and the general bits and pieces that shape people's memories of the Scottish game. In one corner, in a little glass case, is a pair of trainers. Not just any trainers, mind you. It's a pair of trainers worn by a Hibs casual in the 1980s. Your average football follower might be horrified that the footwear of choice of a 1980s hooligan should find its way into the hallowed halls of the Scottish Football museum. They shouldn't be.

Like it or not, casuals are as much a part of Scottish football history as Archie Gemmill's goal against Holland in 1978 or Maurice Johnston's move across the great Glasgow divide in 1989. They have existed longer in senior Scottish football than either Livingston FC or Inverness Caledonian Thistle.

The fact that the shoes are even described as those worn by a casual is remarkable in itself. Back in the 1980s and 1990s, police and clubs alike were quick to decry the use of the word 'casual', preferring instead to refer to the members of casual mobs simply as hooligans. Alistair Darling MP – in a withering condemnation of their violent battles on Edinburgh's streets – even chose to call them common criminals. Yet their very existence as a movement that attracted hundreds of followers is now acknowledged at a stadium that is the focus of Scottish football.

Back in 1986 Bill Anderson, then editor of the Sunday Post, called me into his office to tell me he had a special job for me. He wanted me to go undercover with this new breed of soccer hooligan, the football casual. I told him I'd rather clean his cat's litter tray with my tongue. The prospect of spending my Saturdays caught up in running battles in and around Scotland's football grounds was as appealing as a dose of shingles. I figured the casuals would fade away as quickly as they had sprung up, and could see no logical reason to risk life and limb getting close to them. I also figured they would be a band of savages with precious little regard for their fellow man. I was wrong on both counts.

THESE COLOURS DON'T RUN

While they were no shrinking violets, the casual groups I mixed with were loyal to each other to a fault. The sense of belonging within each group was clearly a draw for many of those who chose to run with a given mob. Dressing to impress was everything. Wear the wrong gear and you'd have been as well supporting the wrong team.

Their code of conduct was also clear. Don't attack the ordinary fan unless he attacks you. Stick to battling with the opposition casuals, who were like-minded people, and, with certain exceptions, would be up for the battle. Simple rules, yet easy to follow.

To my surprise, these were not mindless thugs either. In another life they could have been generals plotting their way around a battlefield. Planning of every trip was done to the nth degree, with precious little left to chance. Neither was their bravery in question. The greatest ignominy for any casual would be the shame of running in the face of the enemy.

None of this is to condone what the casuals did in the Eighties and Nineties. They caused mayhem at football grounds the length and breadth of Britain. Women, children and innocent bystanders did get caught up in that mayhem as fights spilled out of control on to busy shopping streets. Even with the strict guidelines of the casual structure, some ran out of control and lived by their own rules. That handed the authorities the chance to tar them all with the same brush, and it was a chance seized with alarming alacrity.

This book is not intended to be a defence of the actions of the Hibs casuals. Even they would admit that, at times, their actions were indefensible. It is merely a record of what happened, told by a man who was there from day one of the Capital City Service. It is a brutally honest account of the events that saw the CCS grow from a bunch of lads who had gone to football together from their primary-school days into the most-feared casual group in Scotland.

At their peak, they were also one of the most-respected mobs in Britain. Bill Anderson got his way back in 1986 when he sent me out to infiltrate the casuals. He was a man who normally got his way. Some twenty years later, when ZigZag productions asked me to take part in The

*Real Football Factories, a television series looking back at the casual phen-
omenon, I was tempted to ask them if they had an office cat. My time as
an undercover casual had come to a nasty end, with death threats being
phoned to my home. Once that has happened, you tread warily.*

*Another of the contributors to The Real Football Factories was Derek
Dykes, as he outlined how the Capital City Service had operated. When
Fort Publishing's James McCarroll suggested the two of us collaborate on
this book, I once again enquired about his cat's health. The prospect of
revisiting a situation that had ended in such rancour twenty years previously was not one I relished. But instead of finding the devil incarnate
when I visited the home of Derek Dykes, I found a fellow surrounded by
three kids. He was playing happily with them as they tore around the
house as only kids can.*

*Derek's unflinching honesty in revisiting the times and events that
shaped the Capital City Service is the reason this book is what it is, an
accurate, no-punches-pulled look at twenty years of the CCS. No subject,
however painful or embarrassing, has been avoided. No loss of face has
been conveniently forgotten. This is neither the sanitised version of what
went on within the CCS, nor is it merely a catalogue of victorious fights.
If it happened to the CCS, it's included.*

*This is also a tale of a doomed secondary-school romance that was
rekindled in time to rescue one participant, when his life was in tatters.*

*By all means make your own judgements on the actions of the Capital
City Service. But make them once you've read what happened.*

Andy Colvin, July 2007

ACKNOWLEDGEMENTS

In memory of all the boys who are no longer with us. They are all CCS legends and will never be forgotten. Davie Harpol, Stuart Douglas, Steven Gow, Ian Donald, Andy Parker, Deano Cozzi, Horan, Worzel RIP.

Thanks to everyone who made the book possible, especially Andy Colvin for all his hard work. Special thanks to James McCarroll of Fort Publishing Ltd for making this happen. Cheers guys.

Thanks also to the boys who helped with photos and press cuttings: Keggy, Fraser C, Dougie D, Mikey D, Martin. A big thanks to all the Hibs mob past and present for some wonderful times and happy memories.

Special thanks to Donna, Owen, Zoe and Carly for being patient for many hours while Andy and I wrote this book.

Derek Dykes, July 2007

INTRODUCTION

Football hooliganism in Scotland has gone through many different phases. In the 1970s the majority of incidents were alcohol-related. Drunken football fans frequently battled both inside and outside grounds. Bottle throwing was common and, incredible as it seems these days, fans were allowed to bring carry-outs of alcohol into grounds. When full, the cans and bottles provided fuel for the hooligans. When empty, the containers became the weapons. The Seventies had also seen the skinhead fashion in full flow with some clubs having a very small minority who followed the club with the sole intention of causing trouble.

The 'riot' Scottish Cup final of 1980 changed the face of Scottish football forever. Celtic and Rangers fans battled on the pitch at Hampden after a last-minute, extra-time winner by George McCluskey gave Celtic the trophy. Drink was probably not the sole motivating factor as the sectarian divide between the two clubs was frequently the cause of violence. But television pictures of police on horseback racing across the Hampden turf and trying to break up the running battles were beamed around the world.

The Scottish Football Association and the Scottish Office had to be seen to act and the Criminal Justice (Scotland) Act became law, banning not only alcohol inside grounds but also the admission of intoxicated fans. With alcohol no longer the problem in Scotland, a new breed of hooligan was about to be born. The early 1980s heralded the era of the casual. The casual movement was already established in England, with Liverpool setting the trend and Manchester and London catching up. A European Cup-tie between Liverpool and Aberdeen was to transfer the trend to Scotland. It was the first time Scottish fans had clapped eyes on the new get-up for football matches south of the border. Liverpool fans were kitted out in anything but club colours. They had wedge haircuts, leather jackets, expensive trainers. The trend quickly caught on in Aberdeen with Pringle jumpers, Lois cords, Farah and Burberry scarves being the order of the day. The label was the thing, and the more expensive and exclusive the better. During the early 1980s the choice of menswear in most cities was limited to a few big department stores and tracking down obscure tennis shirts became the order of the day for a casual. Fila, Lacoste, Tacchini and Ellesse were the labels of the early Eighties.

Because a lot of the fashion ideas came from abroad, Liverpool's fans were at a huge advantage. Their club were regulars in Europe in the late Seventies and early Eighties thus giving their supporters the chance to shop and thieve their way right across Europe. As the grapevine spread news of the casual phenomenon across the country, a uniform began to emerge. Labels like Slazenger, Lacoste, Ellesse, Burberry, Lois, Kappa, Levi were the order of the day. Anoraks, cords and bleached jeans became a regular sight on the terraces. The trainers were just as important. Sporting the correct footwear was an art form in itself.

Nearly two years after Aberdeen embraced the casual culture, Motherwell were next to pick up the torch. This occurred after a group of their skinheads underestimated the newly-attired Aberdeen Soccer Casuals and dismissed them as 'poofs'. The Motherwell Saturday Service was born. With Motherwell now having a mob of casuals a rivalry quickly developed between them and Aberdeen. By the 1984/85 season casuals had attached themselves to most clubs in Scotland and were regularly making headlines in the newspapers. Fashions changed weekly but labels such as Pringle, Lyle & Scott, Lois, Farah, Ellesse, Fila, Tacchini and·

Diadora had fallen out of style to be replaced by the likes of Armani, Chipie, POP 84, Chevignon and Aquascutum, although Lacoste and Burberry still proved popular. The casual scene had become such a problem that in the early days Motherwell FC even tried to ban fans who were wearing Kappa kagoules from entering the stadium.

By now the Hibs Capital City Service were also on the scene and growing rapidly. The newspapers were paying much greater attention to the casual phenomenon than they ever had to the old football hooligans, who were pretty much seen as ten a penny. The rivalry between Hibs and Aberdeen would last throughout the Eighties and early Nineties and it was both fierce and intense. By that stage Rangers (ICF), Dundee (Utility) and to a lesser extent Celtic (CSC) had also joined the fray while Motherwell's crew diminished in strength. Friendships were being formed with English crews and cross-border trips were commonplace.

The fashions of the Nineties are still in evidence today. Labels popular then were Stone Island, Lacoste, Burberry, Paul Smith, Ralph Lauren and they have been supplemented over the last few years by labels such Massimo Osti, Left Hand, CP Company, Boneville, Paul Smith and Shark.

The early Nineties saw the numbers drop amongst groups of casuals in Scotland with some teams no longer having any hooligan following at all. Hibs and Aberdeen were the only crews to survive in any numbers. The Nineties also saw the police introduce special units to gather intelligence on the casual gangs. Every regional police force in the country had an officer responsible for football intelligence. He would gather information on the groups, such as travel plans for matches and what sort of numbers would be travelling. This had a devastating effect on the hooligan groups, with large numbers being detained before any trouble could break out. Buses were frequently stopped and turned back.

The late Nineties saw a development in the hooligan scene in Scotland, with the formation of the Scottish National Firm (SNF). It caused splits in many crews, particularly Hibs, as people left their original firm to join the new mob. Increased policing, more sophisticated surveillance and a general decline in numbers saw casual violence drop off towards the end of the millennium. A full-on revival of the casual scene in Scotland will probably never happen although recent evidence suggests an upsurge in activity, particularly in Edinburgh. Running battles between Hibs and Hearts crews have taken place in the last twelve months, with police voicing fears that old hands may be training-up a new generation.

A return to the casual levels of the Eighties will not happen. But it would be a fool who supposed the casuals are dead and buried. That mistake was made when casuals first appeared on the scene and were dismissed as a one-season wonder.

That was twenty-five years ago, and they are still around.

1

RAYMIE WAS ALWAYS WITH US

It was 23 March 1985. We were sitting in a pub on Easter Road when we got the shout that Aberdeen had arrived. This was it. Our first major battle on home turf with Scotland's top mob. We had already taken them on, just a few short weeks before, and come up short. But that battle had been outside of Edinburgh. This time we were on familiar territory and we firmly believed we could win.

Looking back on it now in the cold light of day it was madness. It made the Charge of the Light Brigade look like a well-planned military mission. We had about fifty boys and we made our way up to Bothwell Street, where we planned to take them on. Christ, there were hundreds of them. We'd never seen a mob that size in our lives. Our previous experiences of battles at the football were few and far between and even in those our record was mixed. Now, here we were, hopelessly outnumbered and up against the best crew in the country; it was a scrap a blind man could see we couldn't win.

The outcome was inevitable. We did our best but we were up against it from the off and they wound up forcing us to turn and run. It was the only sensible thing to do. But one of our guys,

Raymie Morrell, fell and was surrounded by them. They were like a pack of wolves as they circled him. We were still running but we looked back to see what was happening to Raymie. I don't think I've ever felt so helpless. There was nothing we could do to get him away from them, because there were just so many of them.

As we legged it we figured he'd get a right good kicking and that would be that. But they took liberties, those Aberdeen bastards. Not content with giving him a good doing, they jumped on his head. Not just one boy either, plenty of them. People were even turning back to put the boot in his head a second time, or even a third. They went way over the top. And to make it worse, they even made up a song about it. To the tune of Nena's '99 Red Balloons', they sang:

> *99 soccer reds,*
> *Jumping on poor Raymie's head.*

Sick bastards.

But you know what? They lit a fire in us that day. If the show of power, strength and callousness was meant to scare us off it had the opposite effect. It taught us just how ruthless we would have to be to even the score. And it ensured that, where Aberdeen were concerned, there were now no limits.

Raymie was in a coma for a week and his life was in danger for some time after that before he pulled through. The next time Aberdeen came through he kicked the crap out of one of them in London Road. It was some measure of revenge but nothing like what he'd had done to him.

After that, he never ran with us again and not one of us blamed him. Despite not being there, Raymie Morrell still made his contribution every time we faced Aberdeen. Every time we took on the

Aberdeen Soccer Crew, it was for him. The memory of what had happened to him ensured we never took a backward step.

The Capital City Service was in business.

2

IN THE BEGINNING

The Capital City Service would eventually become a name to strike fear into any soccer mob in Britain. I doubt that in our original guise of Uncle Dougie's Soccer Hooligans we'd have been viewed as being quite as fearsome. Yet that was how it all started out.

I'd been a Hibee since I was a nipper and I used to go to games on the Liberton supporters' bus with a load of my mates. The guy who ran that bus was called Dougie, hence our little gang name. The young boys on the bus were known as Uncle Dougie's Soccer Hooligans and we'd even sing that when we were at games. I suppose that was our first mob chant, if you like. I'd have been about twelve at the time and we were still scarfers then. In other words, we wore the club colours, be it a replica jersey or a club scarf.

Our little gang used to get up to the usual nonsense. On the way to games we'd be shoplifting or nicking stuff from service stations whenever the bus stopped. There was no violence then, we were too young. At that time, our little mob was all guys from Leith, from our local area. But just by going to the games regularly you'd bump into boys from all over Edinburgh who'd come on their supporters' buses. I'd meet guys from Niddrie, Tollcross, Granton, from all over the city. As the years went by and you saw the same faces, you became good mates with them.

Let's face it, we had a common cause. We were Hibees and proud of it. We were also proud of our city, the capital of Scotland. If you were drawing a template for the archetypal football casual, it was us. Pride in your team, pride in your city. We just didn't realise it at the time and, to be fair, when I was that young the casual movement hadn't really started. But given the qualities required to be a casual, you might imagine a slur against Hibs or against Edinburgh would have been the spark that lit the fire for the formation of the CCS. It wasn't. It was a mindless act of violence and it was in Airdrie of all places.

Hibs were due to play a League Cup tie on 30 November 1983 at Airdrie's Broomfield ground, a real tip of a stadium but one that generated a fantastic atmosphere. I don't know why we even bothered going to the game because it was a meaningless fixture. Neither of the two teams could qualify from their group and Airdrie in midweek is not going to make it on to any list of travel hot spots. But we were Hibees and we were daft and it was something to do.

The problem with going to Airdrie was that their ground wasn't the best for getting in and out of. And it just so happened they had a bunch of nutters among their support known as the Section B boys. These fellas were handy and were known among football fans around Scotland as a group to be respected. They were skinheads and more typical of the football hooligan of the time. They also treated Broomfield as if they owned it and visiting fans going there had to be on their toes to avoid getting a Doc Marten print on their coupons.

The local coppers were alert to the Section B mob and kept

them in the ground until visiting fans had got out. It didn't stop you running the gauntlet, though, and that night was no different. As we made to leave the Section B mob charged at us and we had to leg it out of the gate before the cops got them back under control. We made our way back to the bus and waited on everyone else arriving so we could get back to Edinburgh.

But the local constabulary in their infinite wisdom let the Section B mob out before the last of the visiting fans had got on their buses. The coaches were a sitting target and one the skinheads didn't miss. They appeared out of nowhere and set about tanning the windows on our bus. Don't ask my why, because to this day I couldn't tell you, but Uncle Dougie's Soccer Hooligans were suddenly all grown up and they weren't having it.

We piled off the bus, set about the Section B and forced the skinheads to beat a tactical retreat. That was us; we thought we were the bee's knees. We figured we were big and brave because we'd chased, and seen off, a bunch of skinheads. By the time the local coppers ambled along to see what all the fuss was about, word had already got out about what we'd done. Other buses got to hear about it and, as I said, we really thought we were it.

Within a matter of months of that incident the papers were starting to run stuff about casuals and we decided that's what we would be. Somehow it seemed different from being a football hooligan and we reckoned we had what it took to cut it as casuals. In terms of the people I hung around with, it didn't make a blind bit of difference whether we were casuals or not.

All the guys who decided to be casuals were people I'd been going to football with since I was twelve or thirteen, but the idea of becoming a casual seemed to draw even more people together. That's how the Hibs mob drew folk from everywhere because we'd all been going to football before that.

In the beginning we were formed mainly from the Liberton, Granton, Tollcross and Leith buses but the rest eventually caught up. We all hung about with each other during the week, as well as at the football on a Saturday, because first and foremost we were mates. But it had an immediate effect on our trips to Easter Road because we were shunned by the ordinary fans from the off. Aberdeen's mob were running riot at the time and the Motherwell Saturday Service were also on the loose. The press were having a field day and in their usual measured way they were describing casuals as if they were the spawn of Satan. Tales of rampaging bands of savages coming to a town near you filled column inches and were accompanied by screaming headlines.

Unsurprisingly, the casuals didn't mind the coverage because it enhanced their reputation rather than destroying it. But the cops and the clubs seized on the coverage and used it to try and turn the ordinary, decent fan away from this new breed of hooligan. Hibs scarfers, in particular, were very vocal in their opposition to casuals in the beginning. You have no idea how uncomfortable it can feel to be standing in Easter Road, your home ground, with your new mob and you're kitted out in your bleached jeans, Nike Wimbledon trainers and a Nike or Adidas kagoule. And while you're feeling like a million dollars in your gear, thousands of people are singing 'Oh, it's magic, you know, Hibees and casuals don't go' and they're singing directly at you. These were people we'd stood shoulder to shoulder with on many an away terracing. Now, we were standing shoulder to cold shoulder with them. We were well out on a limb.

The only consolation was that, as the days and weeks went by, more and more people got in touch to say they wanted to join the mob until we had a band of about fifty. And we had a name. We'd toyed with the idea of calling ourselves 'The Family' because that's what it felt like within our mob but it sounded too nice. We still sang 'The Hibees family' to the tune of *The Addams Family* whenever we were on the march but it was no name for a mob.

So Capital City Service it was but, to be honest, it really didn't look like happening for us in the beginning. When we became casuals we didn't have a clue what we were doing. We knew what clothes to wear but we didn't really grasp the concept of the fighting. We weren't the biggest crew and we weren't even the bravest of mobs back then.

* * *

But we were ambitious. We wanted to be number one. And to become number one we had to take on, and defeat, the mob at the top of the tree: Aberdeen. That was why we embarked on the most ridiculous mission of them all in February 1985. Aberdeen had been drawn to play away at Raith Rovers in the Scottish Cup, by which time we had been knocked out of the competition. It was a long haul for the Aberdeen mob to Kirkcaldy, a short train ride across the Forth rail bridge for us. On the face of it, perfect for us. In reality, a suicide mission.

We checked out the train timetable and opted to take the latest possible train to get to Raith's Stark's Park in time for kick-off. We didn't want to take on Aberdeen outside the ground where we figured their numerical advantage would mean that we copped a hiding. We also figured there would be coppers aplenty escorting the Aberdeen mob from the railway station. Raith didn't have a mob but nobody would take the chance that Aberdeen would run riot through Kirkcaldy. They were cocky bastards and they loved the notion that they were untouchable.

There was also the fact that we really didn't know the area round Stark's Park all that well. We didn't know the rat runs, the escape routes, the streets to be avoided because they'd bring you straight back into trouble. Bearing all that in mind, we'd decided an attack outside the ground was a non-starter. The plan was to launch an attack inside the ground and catch them unawares.

On the day of the match we assembled a mob of about fifty and made our way to Waverley. By the time the train reached Kirkcaldy everyone was pumped up. And we'd timed it perfectly. By our reckoning, by the time we made our way from the station to the ground Aberdeen would be inside, oblivious to the fact we were on our way to sort them out. You know what? There was almost a swagger about us as we made our way through Kirkcaldy. The Raith scarfers were wondering what the fuck was going on. They'd already ducked into doorways and shops when Aberdeen had come strolling through their town. Now there was another mob and they had no idea who we were. They weren't about to stop and ask. They kept their heads down and kept moving.

And that's what we did. We kept moving, kept walking, with the pace picking up and getting brisker the closer we got to Stark's Park. Once we reached our destination the plan was simple. For all it was a cup-tie it was pay at the gate. Stark's Park was a lot bigger in those days and there would be no problem fitting the crowd in. We'd pay in to the visiting end, slip in among a bunch of Aberdeen scarfers and locate the Aberdeen mob. Then we'd launch our attack and take them by surprise. If it all went to plan, bingo!

Put like that, it really wasn't a bad plan and all was going perfectly as we turned into the street that takes you up to Stark's Park. And, in that instant, we realised the glaring flaw in our surprise mission. The street running up to the ground goes straight up because Stark's Park sits on top of a hill, looking out over the seafront and the esplanade at Kirkcaldy. The terracing that housed the away support was steeply banked and fans stood at the back could see up and down that street. And that's where the Aberdeen mob had taken up their position. It was almost as if they were expecting us. By the time we'd paid in and made our way up the embankment all we could see was a sea of them charging at us. All our planning and strategies went out of the window in that instant because they were on us before we even had a chance to get ready for them.

It was every man for himself and it was a fight to survive.

I managed to catch a quick glimpse of the pitch before the first blow hit me. That was it. It was all-out war. They were swinging and nutting and booting and we were doing likewise. There was no way we were running but it didn't make a blind bit of difference because we were badly outnumbered. It was only a matter of time before the extra numbers on their side told but at least we were sticking together as a mob.

My last memory of that battle is tumbling down the terracing, arse over tip, with boots going into my ribs and head. You'd no sooner sucked up the pain from one blow when another one arrived and the terracing I was tumbling down wasn't exactly a featherbed either. At some point I must have passed out because when I came round I was on the pitch being treated. Along with another guy from our mob I was taken away in an ambulance to be checked over in hospital while the rest of the CCS were marched out of the ground by the coppers. They were escorted all the way back to the station by a large contingent of Fife's finest and put on the train.

But our guys were nothing if not resourceful. They found a load of bottles and smuggled them onto the train, knowing the coppers wouldn't escort them all the way back to Edinburgh. All the police wanted was for us to be out of their town. So the boys were on the train with this load of bottles and they'd reckoned on something the coppers hadn't. The railway line back to Edinburgh runs right along-side Stark's Park and it sits above the level of the terracing wall.

As the train drew alongside the ground one of the boys pulled the communication cord and the driver stopped. The boys opened the windows on the train doors and started hurling bottles into the Aberdeen end at their mob. They said you could see wee spaces appearing among the Aberdeen mob every time a bottle landed and smashed in the middle of them. Aberdeen's mob were raging because there was nothing they could do. They couldn't climb the terracing wall to get at our boys because there were coppers appearing from everywhere. By the time the driver was ordered to get the train moving we'd at least achieved a little victory, even if it wasn't the one we'd hoped for. And it was nice to know that it wasn't only our plan that had a huge hole in it, but also the coppers' evacuation plan. They'd given our boys a second chance to have a go and that gave us some extra pleasure.

Of course, at this time I was oblivious to the fact the CCS had achieved any sort of victory on the day. Me and the other fella were getting poked and prodded by doctors as they tried to determine if there were any broken bones. Fortunately, there weren't; just bruises and dented egos and the doctors couldn't do anything about the latter. There was the odd cut and scrape as well and they patched us up before discharging us.

We caught a taxi from the hospital to the station but while our timing in arriving at the station on the way to Kirkcaldy had been perfect, our timing on departure was horrible. We'd lost all track of time and hadn't even realised we'd been in the hospital for a couple of hours. Guess what? A football match lasts ninety minutes and, even allowing for the hold-up for the bottle-throwing, it had finished about twenty minutes earlier.

The taxi had just pulled up at the station when a load of police came round the corner. We figured we'd been rumbled and were about to spend a night in the cells when we realised they were just the advance party. The main body of coppers then appeared escorting the two-hundred-strong Aberdeen mob we'd scrapped with earlier. My mate was already halfway out of the taxi when I grabbed his jacket, hauled him back in, and pointed silently at the Aberdeen mob. It was like a comedy film. The two of us screamed 'Drive!' at the cabbie at exactly the same time. 'Where to?' he asked. 'Anywhere,' we replied. 'Just get us away from the station.'

To be fair him he didn't take liberties. He could have driven round and round and jacked up the price because he knew he had a captive audience. We weren't going anywhere until we knew Aberdeen were safely on a train and on their way home. Walking into that station with them there would have been suicide. They'd have been well up for a second go and there were only two of us. Bear in mind we were also blissfully unaware about the bottle-throwing at that point. They'd have torn us limb from limb just to finish the job.

But the taxi driver was a good guy. He settled for driving us a wee bit down the street, and he dropped us off under a railway bridge. We paid him and bunged him a decent tip and he told us the next train we heard heading north would be the one the Aberdeen fans were on. Once we'd heard that, it would be safe for us to head back to the station. And that's exactly what we did. We hid under that bridge, smoking fags and keeping an eye out until we heard the train pass over above our heads.

Then we broke cover and skulked back into the station, still checking right and left to make sure there were no stragglers. By the time we caught a train back to Edinburgh and headed for the pub the boys' spirits had at least been raised by the bottle-throwing. We'd made some mark on the day, although to be fair the marks causing me concern were the bruises starting to appear on my body.

Of equal concern was the fact that despite achieving something on the day, we'd been tactically naive. We'd put ourselves into a no-win situation. Quite simply, if we were ever going to get the better of Aberdeen we had to improve. And quickly. But little did we realise that the worst day in the history of the CCS was just around the corner.

And that Aberdeen would again be our tormentors.

3

PLANNING FOR SUCCESS

We were numb after the Raymie incident. There wasn't much laughing and joking as we made our way to Easter Road for the game. Even the scarfers had heard what had happened and some of them were asking us if the lad was OK. The bottom line was we didn't know. We couldn't even tell them how our mate was.

By half-time the Chinese whispers inside Easter Road were in overdrive. There was a general buzz around the ground that Raymie had died. And then there was the Aberdeen mob, up at the fence baiting us. God, how we hated them that day. The problem was there was another group we hated just as much and that was ourselves. We'd got ourselves into the situation and now for all we knew one of our mates could be dead.

To be fair to the scarfers, they were raging with the Aberdeen mob as well and for the whole of the second half, the atmosphere inside Easter Road was horrible. It was truly poisonous. For most of the game a hail of missiles rained down not only on the Aberdeen mob but also on the Aberdeen players. You name it, Hibs fans threw it; bottles, stones and coins from the scarfers; iron bolts and golf balls courtesy of the CCS. If memory serves I think a couple of Aberdeen players were hit and also one of the match officials.*

The coppers had anticipated that there might be some kind of revenge attack on the Aberdeen mob after the match because they had a massive presence outside the ground. You could barely see Aberdeen for the black uniforms surrounding them. With that size of escort to get them back to Waverley station, payback was not on the menu that night, although God knows we tried. It would have been better if it had been, even if we'd copped a doing, because our only other option was to go to the pub. A deflated, defeated, bitter army trooped into the boozer and it wasn't long before the recriminations started. It was little wonder that we were at each other's throats; within the space of a few weeks Aberdeen had given us two hidings, the first at Kirkcaldy, and now this, right in the heart of our city.

It wasn't even drink-fuelled because we'd barely taken a sip of our first pint before the arguments started. One guy was pointing the finger at another, saying 'You ran.' Back came the reply. 'No I fucking didn't. You ran.' They'd been mates for years but it wasn't personal. It was frustration and embarrassment, pure and simple, and in a way it was good to see. If we'd all headed off to the pub

---

* It was every bit as bad as Dykes remembers. The match referee told the *Sunday Mail* that the scenes in the ground were the worst he had ever witnessed. Aberdeen goalkeeper Jim Leighton was hit in the neck by an iron bolt and his teammate Alex McLeish by a coin. One of the unfortunate linesmen was struck on the head by a stone, at which point the referee stopped the game until a semblance of order was restored. The *Sunday Mail* of 24 March 1985 devoted almost its whole back page to the crowd violence, under the headline 'Thug Rule is Back'.

and not given a toss about what had happened a few hours earlier, the mob would have been finished from the off. At least there was still that spark, that fire. We'd been humbled on our own patch, lost a good man in the process, and we had to regroup.

But at the end of the day you couldn't say one guy ran and another one stood. On this particular day we all ran. The blame game had to stop and we had to focus on what was important – how we went forward from there. Once tempers had calmed down we were all in agreement on one thing and that was it could never happen again. First of all we had to face up to the fact that we were still innocents abroad. You could have told us to go up and stand beside a copper that day and flick V-signs at Aberdeen and we'd have thought that made us casuals. Half of us probably hadn't even been in a fight at the football before so it was all totally new. But, once Raymie was almost kicked to death, that was when the penny dropped and it all became a lot more organised and a lot more serious.

The Raymie incident changed everything. Once that happened it was all about revenge. There was no shame in losing that battle to Aberdeen because the one thing you learn over the years is that no mob wins every battle. You have to take your kickings. Up until then we'd thought it was all about the boys being together and having a bit of a laugh and wearing the gear. But that day against Aberdeen truly brought it home to us that it wasn't a laugh. It was serious and, quite literally, a matter of life and death. Our world had changed forever.

First up we had to get a structure in place to make sure we were properly organised the next time we went into battle. When we'd faced Aberdeen we were a shambles, there's no other way to describe it. That had to change. Most casual mobs had a top boy but that wasn't the way we ran things in the CCS. We didn't see the need for one guy to call the shots because a lot of us had grown up together. In all the time I was with Hibs, we never had a top boy.

A command structure of five guys was put in place – myself, Scott, Sean, Ian and Bri – although we didn't think of ourselves as commanders. We were more like organisers or planners. From then on we would meet up during the week and discuss what was going to happen at the next game. We would plan everything to the last detail. Our group would take the decisions on where we were leaving from, what time we were leaving, what route we were going to take, who was going to go where and what we were going to do when we got there. Each of the five guys making up that group were selected because they were game, they had bottle.

Believe me: that group of five were game, game guys and I'm not just blowing my own trumpet because I was one of them. We weren't necessarily the best fighters or anything like that. We were simply people who were respected within the mob. That was how we ran things. You didn't have to be the best fighter but you had to be a leader. At the end of the day there were a lot of people who went to football who were a lot harder than me, no question about that. I've never claimed to be a brilliant fighter or a hard man; I'm neither of those things. But for all the hard guys both in our mob and in other mobs, I'm willing to bet there weren't many who were more game than me and I'm happy to bum myself up about that.

Ultimately, that was what earned you respect, being game and being up for a scrap when it came your way. You could be the biggest, toughest guy in the world, the sort of guy who has muscles in his spit. But even with all those advantages you could still be a coward and run when it all kicked off. Me? Back then I weighed in at about ten stone with a wet dufflecoat on but I was always game, I was always in when there was a fight. I always made sure I was in and I would never run.

The Raymie incident forced us to rethink our strategy when it came to the fight itself. We cottoned on almost immediately to the fact we were in trouble from the off because we'd just charged up the road towards Aberdeen like a bunch of idiots. Their mob must have been loving it when they saw us running towards them like headless chickens. I didn't know who was on my right, I didn't know who was on my left, I didn't know who was behind me. It was a disorganised rabble and that was how Raymie had become isolated.

From that day on we fought with a simple system where the battle lines were selected beforehand. You always made sure you had two or three lines of game boys so you knew who was alongside you and you knew who was behind you, over both shoulders. You knew that if you were in, they were in there with you and they weren't leaving you if things turned ugly. They weren't leaving you under any circumstances. If a man went down, the next line simply pushed forward so that he could be rescued rather than being left to the mercy of the mob. It was a case of, 'Right. We're forming the first line, you're forming the second line, you're forming the third line.' I was in the first line, the front line if you like, and I knew all of the guys on that line and they knew me.

That familiarity with each other from way back meant we would stand together. All the pals stayed together and you knew then that there was no chance of anyone getting left. I know it might sound a bit too regimented and you would think there might have been some gripes about it but there weren't. It was quite easy to get it through to people and the guys took it on board from the off. Raymie's situation saw to that.

We had a tendency to have a group of twenty in front of the others, nutters who would start everything and the rest would need to catch up. I was one of those twenty and we were often way up the road ahead of the rest. On the face of it we were ignoring our own plans but we still stuck to that system of battle lines, even within the little group of twenty. And when there are twenty of you, you know your back is covered. With those two measures in place, at least there was a bit more organisation and structure to what we were trying to do. It wasn't just, 'Let's go and have a tear up' because we'd learned a very hard way it wasn't as simple as that. It would be a mistake to think those simple measures turned the CCS into a successful mob overnight. It took probably a season, or perhaps a season-and-a-half, on a pretty steep learning curve, before we absolutely knew what we were doing.

Over the years we added even more refinements to the battle plan. When ambushing a mob we'd strike them in the middle of the group. It wasn't just about trying to split them into two groups; it was much more cynical than that. We knew from experience that the really game boys were up at the front and at the rear, both to lead the attack, and to cover the back of the group. With most mobs, the guys in the middle were the ones who liked the idea of running with a group, but weren't too keen on getting their hands dirty or their heads bashed. They were the easiest ones to get running. It was the law of the jungle. Prey on the weak first.

We also had to devise ways of outwitting the coppers. There are police escorts to get opposition mobs safely from the station or from their buses. They were normally positioned at the back and at the front as the away mob walked to Easter Road. So what we would do was send a group out ahead of the escort and have another group to the rear. The group in front would start trouble and the cops from the back would rush forward to help their colleagues. That left the back of the opposition mob unprotected and we'd steam in before the cops could regroup. That particular tactic worked a treat because it meant a lot of their best boys were stranded up front surrounded by cops and CCS while we set about the rest of their mob.

But it was also the case that we didn't get two hundred bodies overnight. Another problem was that, of the new boys who came in, we didn't know who the game ones were for a long time. But the one thing the Raymie incident did was to galvanise people. The Aberdeen Soccer Crew had acted as recruiting sergeants for us without even realising it because people were so disgusted by what they'd done, by the liberty they'd taken.

There was no shortage of bodies the next time we played Aberdeen at Easter Road. It seemed as if every nutter in Edinburgh wanted a pop at the cowards. They were appearing from everywhere and we couldn't believe it. As soon as Aberdeen were due in town we had people offering to join us in their droves. We'd done some recruiting ourselves and it wasn't that difficult to get people along, given the circumstances. You'd talk to some of your mates who weren't running with the CCS and say to them: 'These are the bastards who did Raymie.' You didn't need to say another word. The look in their eyes told you they were in. Revenge is a powerful recruiting tool. Once they'd tasted action for the first time, they were generally hooked.

If they weren't hooked, they probably weren't much use to us anyway. People who didn't enjoy the battle weren't the sort of game guys we needed and, when you're building up a mob, you can't afford to carry passengers. You're either in, or you're out. Fortunately most of them enjoyed the day so much they decided they'd come again the next week, the nutters especially. They'd finally found an outlet for all that pent-up aggression. That was how the CCS built up from a small bunch of wannabes to the top firm in Scotland.

It didn't do us any harm, either, that the next time we faced Aberdeen we found ourselves splashed all over the front pages of the newspapers; but more of that later. Notoriety is no bad thing when you're trying to get noticed and a lot of people who were there for the first time that day basked in the glory of being able to tell their mates they'd been part of it. Cue another influx of volunteers the following week, and so it went on.

But if one thing made the CCS unique it was the make-up of our mob. There was the original forty or fifty who'd been going to Hibs games for years but we also had people from other teams. There were Celtic fans, Rangers fans and, would you believe it, even Hearts boys over the years. At the end of the day they were all Hibs casuals, if you know what I mean. That mix made our mob different but it also made it a whole lot of fun to be around.

I really don't think the scarfers knew what to make of us because of the cross-section of fans within our group. You'd have the Celtic fans in our crew standing on the terracing at Easter Road singing Irish rebel songs and right behind them you'd have the Rangers boys singing 'God Save the Queen'. It goes without saying the Hearts boys weren't allowed to sing. They'd have got a kicking from us and from the scarfers. But the banter was brilliant. After the initial doings from Aberdeen we felt that we'd never laugh again.

Now we were all smiles.

4

FAINT HEARTS

I know it might seem surprising to some people that we had Hearts boys in our crew but, I'll tell you what, if ever a bunch of boys proved their bottle just by joining us it was them. They weren't like the Celtic or Rangers guys, who just happened to be Old Firm fans living in Edinburgh and wanted a mob to run with. The twenty Hearts boys who joined us had been casuals, our cross-town enemies and sworn rivals. It took massive bottle for them to front up at Easter Road and stand beside us.

You can imagine the reception they got from some of our crew and that was understandable too. When somebody smacks you in the kisser, then comes strolling up wanting to be a friend, you're more likely to shake him warmly by the throat than by the hand. They got an awful lot of stick, an awful lot, and the Hearts boys weren't sure how to handle it. We told them straight that if they were serious about joining us they just had to put up with the initial hostility and eventually everything would calm down. Normally, within a couple of weeks, it did, although there were guys in our crew who were always chipping away at them.

It was all, 'We can never trust you, you're Hearts' but in the end we told them to leave it out because it wasn't doing anyone any good. In the end they got accepted because they were game guys and they got stuck in whenever there was a battle to be fought. You can't ask for any more than that from any member of your mob.*

To be fair, you couldn't blame the Hearts boys for wanting to join us because their own crew was a disgrace. The boys who joined us were sick of getting kickings from Hibs. The Hearts mob were cowards, pure and simple. There's no other word to describe them. And they were definitely the second-class citizens when it came to Edinburgh soccer crews. We ran the city and we terrorised Hearts. Every time we were coming back from an away game we'd get off the train at Haymarket station, the stop before ours at Waverley. That's because it was bang in the centre of Hearts territory. They drank in the Haymarket bar, which sat directly across the road from the station. And every time we'd come out of the station, tear across the road to that bar, put the windows in, kick the doors in, pile inside, start dragging them about and give them a kicking.

In the end I don't know who was more surprised when that happened. Them, that we kept on doing it, or us, that they were stupid enough to keep on going there whenever they knew we'd be coming back from an away game. You'd have thought the penny

---

* This unholy alliance was highlighted by the *Edinburgh Evening News* in its edition of 15 October 1990. In an interview with someone described as a '22-year-old unemployed labourer' the paper notes that, 'He is one of the leading Hibs casuals yet he is a Hearts fan!' The 'convert' spoke freely to the *News* of his 'Jekyll and Hyde' existence and explained that he had gone over to the other side because 'Hearts casuals would not stand – they had no back up.' He also admitted being part of the two-hundred-strong mob of CCS that had travelled to London to take on Millwall's notorious mob. AC

would have dropped at some point. It would have been different if they'd offered any sort of resistance but it was minimal. It was like one of those old Westerns where the bandits run the town and sweep in whenever it suits them. The difference was that Hearts didn't have a sheriff in a white hat to save them.

Because Hearts were based in the west of the city and Hibs were based in the east, Princes Street was almost the halfway point but we were in control of that. And even when we got bored in Princes Streeet there was no let up for Hearts. We'd go down to Gorgie, which should have been a no-go area for us because that was meant to be solid Hearts territory, but they did nothing to defend it. We were chasing them through Gorgie night after night and that's where their team's ground is. It would have been unthinkable to us that they could chase us around Easter Road or Leith yet they wouldn't even defend their own patch.

We hung around outside the Wimpy burger bar in Princes Street and we had someone there from ten in the morning to midnight. There was normally a good fifty or sixty CCS there at night and the staff were terrified of us. It got to the point that if we went in with an order for burgers or fries they would give us the food for nothing just to keep us sweet. Then we moved down to the Wimpy in the west end of the city, once again in Hearts territory, and I think Hearts just got sick of it. They were petrified of us and that's why their more game boys joined us. They wanted to be part of a mob that meant something.

The whole twenty didn't come at once; they joined up in threes and fours. They were advised about what to expect and warned that if they walked away over the initial abuse they'd get then they weren't what we wanted anyway. We told them straight that if someone wanted to even a score by smacking them in the face and they accepted it and walked away there was no way back with us. If, on the other hand, they got smacked in the face and had a go back, then turned up again the next week, that would be different altogether. That showed bottle, and these boys had plenty of it.

And as time goes on, and you're standing shoulder to shoulder with them in fights, they become accepted. At the end of the day, as long as they weren't in the Hibs end at a derby game, jumping up and down when Hearts scored, they were fine by us. Those must have been the hardest days for those boys because it wasn't as if they could opt not to turn up for Hibs–Hearts games. They had to be there. If they didn't turn up on that day, there was no way back for them. I'll tell you something else. We put them right up front on those days and they didn't flinch. The point was they knew they wouldn't get any backlash from Hearts because they had us backing them up. One phone call and there would be fifty of us there in no time at all.

The thing was that Hearts liked the idea of being a soccer crew, but didn't much like the idea of what it entailed. Back then we dished out hidings, they were good at hiding. Before an Edinburgh derby we'd call them up and say: 'We're here, where are you?' That's how it was done. You're in one place, the other mob's somewhere else and you wind up meeting in the middle. But we'd call them up and they'd say 'We're not coming today.' That's not the point of the game. The point is you meet up and battle.

So once they started that nonsense we had to change tack on derby days at Tynecastle. We'd march right up Gorgie Road from Haymarket, going into every pub to look for them. We rarely found them. They were hiding again. We'd have had more chance of finding Lord Lucan and Shergar. In those days we had to come down McLeod Street after the game and you normally ran into the Hearts scarfers round about there. They were always well up for it, they put their casuals to shame. The scarfers called themselves the

Gorgie Aggro and they always had a go. Imagine a bunch of casuals hiding behind their scarfers. On their home patch as well!

It got to the stage that we had to find out where they were going to meet up before the game and get there first, just to force them to fight. One time we found out they were meeting in the Wheatsheaf pub at the far end of Gorgie Road. It's at Saughton Park, and it was about as far way from us as they could get while still staying in their area. If they'd been any further away they'd have needed passports. All we did was set off early that morning. As soon as the Wheatsheaf opened its doors we were in, the whole mob of us. We filled the place and it was heaving. When Hearts turned up and opened the door the looks on their faces said it all. We poured out of the pub and gave them a right doing. At least they stood and fought, even if it had been forced on them. The landlord of the Wheatsheaf must have been cursing us, though, because I don't think the Hearts mob went back there for a long time.

The only problem with giving them that doing was that it made them even more reluctant to face us. Before another derby at Tynecastle we were tipped-off that they were meeting at Strathie's, in Gorgie Road. It opened early in the morning so we were in there by ten o'clock, mob-handed as usual. You know what Hearts did? They went by on the top deck of a bus, peering out of the windows to see if it was safe to come in for a pint. And when they clocked us in Strathie's, they stayed on the bus. Cowards.

No, when we went to Tynecastle it was the Gorgie Aggro who gave it a go and they were well known as a bunch of nutters. They used to give Hibs scarfers some right bad doings because the location of Tynecastle makes it difficult to get away from. When I was a kid going to games Hibs scarfers had to leave derby matches at Tynecastle ten minutes from the end to avoid a kicking. There's a bus stop right outside the ground at what used to be the away end and the bus back to the other side of the city always arrived before the game finished. If you didn't catch that one, you were stuck in Gorgie Road and when the Aggro came pouring round from McLeod Street you were a sitting duck.

The Aggro took on two hundred of us in 1985 and we wound up chasing them right down Gorgie Road and into Fountain Road. It was brilliant. They were running for their lives and we were hot on their heels. So much for the Gorgie Aggro. We caught up with them, gave them the hiding they'd deserved for years of terrorising Hibs fans and even got away before the cops came. And, from what I heard, Hibs scarfers didn't get much hassle from the Aggro from then on.

I just didn't understand the Hearts casuals back then and even now I don't get what they were all about. They turned out for every other mob that came to Edinburgh. They took on Celtic, Aberdeen, Rangers, Motherwell, but they wouldn't front up for us. From 1984 until I gave it up in 2003 they walked up to Easter Road twice. Twice!

The first time, in 1987, they gave it a go and they didn't even make it beyond the east end of Princes Street. We ambushed them there and they came off a poor second best. That obviously had an effect on them because they left it another sixteen years before deciding to try again. Then, in 2003, they actually made it to the top of Easter Road. We were probably caught off guard by the idea of Hearts walking on our patch. Didn't make much difference in the end. Once we caught up with them, we annihilated them.

In the years in between Hearts would still turn up at the derby games but they came by taxi. They'd get dropped off at the ground, get inside as quickly as they could, then come up to the fence that separated the opposing fans. That was where we always stood so they knew where to find us. So they'd stand there, all brave behind the fence, and hurl abuse. We'd tell them we'd see them after the game and they'd be up for it. And then you'd get outside and they were nowhere to be seen. They were probably back in the Wheatsheaf. With the doors bolted.

I had no respect at all for Hearts as a mob. They were an embarrassment to casuals. But I had plenty of respect for the good boys we got from them and one of them had every reason to thank his Hearts background while in a battle with us. We were scrapping with Leeds in London Road when he got nicked by a copper, who chucked him into a van. The copper had spotted him running along London Road as the battle kicked off and, quite rightly, reckoned he was one of us. But he told this copper, 'You've got it all wrong, pal, I was just an innocent bystander.' The copper was having none of it until he said, 'Honest mate, I'm a Hearts fan' and rolled up his sleeve to show him his tattoo. It reads, 'Hearts, Scottish Cup winners, 1998' and has the Hearts crest on it. The bloke had it done to commemorate their victory over Rangers in the final that year. The copper saw the tattoo and figured there was no way a Hearts fan was going to be fighting alongside Hibs, so he let him go.

Tell you what, that Hearts tattoo saw more casual action than any of the Hearts casuals ever did.

* * *

Hearts fans weren't the only additions to our crew in the early days because although we'd suffered some setbacks we were gaining momentum and building in size. Guys were talking their pals into running with us. And the more folk you attract, the more word of mouth spreads the message and brings in even more foot soldiers.

Some guys had even brought their young brothers along to see what it was all about. Now that's the quickest recruiting tool of the lot. Young guys at fourteen or fifteen want to be part of a mob, they want to feel tough. And once you get a few of them coming along, they go back to school and bum to their mates about what they did and what they saw at the weekend and before you know it you're overrun with the wee buggers.

In 1985 it was a situation that had to be carefully managed for some very simple reasons. The youngsters weren't of an age where they could come into pubs with us, either before games or when we were meeting up during the week to plan our next battle. That meant they hung about outside the boozer and that was far from ideal. By then there were so many of them, all dressed in the gear, that whenever we were in a pub there was a small crowd gathered outside. We'd have been as well putting up a neon sign saying 'CCS meeting in progress. Coppers not welcome.' It was bad enough during the week but on a match day the last thing we wanted was the coppers seeing a band of youngsters outside whatever pub we were in, because that would be the action done for the day. The sole reason we were able to get a battle in the first place was because we were one step ahead of the coppers. Advertising our whereabouts was not part of the plan.

So the youngsters had to be managed and in the end the solution was simple. They needed their own identity, one that didn't draw attention to us. That was why we formed a baby crew, almost like a CCS youth team. They still fought alongside us on Saturdays, to all intents and purposes they were CCS, but they didn't hang around the pubs we were in. While we were in the boozer, they were in McDonald's or Burger King or a local café.

They had their own name, too. The Hibs manager at the time was John Blackley so the baby crew became known as the BBC, Blackley's Baby Crew. I'm not sure how a Hibs legend felt about having a group of casuals named after him. I should imagine he wasn't overly chuffed. But the BBC was born and a really game wee guy called Brad had the job of organising them. I think Brad was only fifteen at the time but he was a natural leader and, as a boxer, a natural when it came to the business end on match days as well.

When you think about it, what we'd done was set up the CCS like a football club. Blackley's Baby Crew was our youth system and whenever they were old enough to get into pubs, they stepped into the full CCS. In years to come they would coach the next generation of the Baby Crew. It guaranteed a steady stream of youngsters for the CCS.

And they were game wee guys as well. We were young and daft. They were even younger, and equally as daft. The words *backward* and *step* clearly weren't in their vocabulary and that's why we had to take another leaf out of football's coaching manual. The youngsters needed training, not of the physical-fitness variety, but of the streetwise variety.

So Sunday nights became training nights. Plenty of visitors to Edinburgh will have parked in King's Stables Road car park. It sits in the shadow of Edinburgh Castle and is just off Lothian Road. It was also the university from which Blackley's Baby Crew graduated. On Sunday nights the BBC would make their way to King's Stables Road and members of the CCS would meet them there.

The youngsters were taught our rules and strategies, our battle plans. We'd made our rookie mistakes, and kids at fourteen or fifteen are even more likely to rush in where angels fear to tread than the older guys who were supposedly meant to know better. That's what Sunday nights were all about but at this school of hard knocks there was no written test, only a practical one. They'd learn the tactics we employed, then go and put them into practice. They'd also have to prove they were physically up to it. It might sound cruel, it might even sound like bullying, but no one was forced to come along and no one was forced to go through with it if they didn't fancy it. Any one of them could walk away at any time if they felt they were in over their heads, and there were some who did just that. There were no recriminations against those who walked away.

The training wasn't subtle. Basically, we'd get one of the Baby Crew to run at two or three of the CCS. They had to give it their best shot and we wouldn't hold back in sorting them out. I'm not talking physical damage here; no one ended up in the hospital or suffered broken bones or even cuts. It was about teaching them that, while running with a mob might seem like a load of fun and a right good laugh, when people hit you it hurts. They were far better off discovering that in King's Stables Road car park on a Sunday night than at Pittodrie or Ibrox or Parkhead or Fir Park.

You don't want to be doing your homework in the heat of battle. You need to know your stuff from the off, or you fail the biggest exam of them all. Or, to go back to the football analogy, you don't pitch a bunch of rookies into the biggest match of the season. Once the BBC kids had gone at two or three of us, one of us would go at two or three of them. Depending on how generous we were feeling, two of us would sometimes go at ten of them. Not too often, mind you. As I said, these were game wee buggers and they knew how to dish it out. There was more than one Sunday night when, if it had been a boxing match, the BBC might have been in with a shout of a win on points and the big boys were the ones nursing bruised faces. And the youngsters weren't slow in giving it the verbals when that was the case. They loved sticking it to the older guys. They were always hyped up on a Sunday night.

But there was more to it than just slugging it out with each other. They had to know when enough was enough, and I know that sounds rich coming from a bunch of guys who'd once waded blindly into Stark's Park and copped a doing for their recklessness. That's what I meant about the learning curve. There was no point in their inexperience leading them to make the same mistakes we had, when we could make them a better, more disciplined, more solid unit. We taught them how to cover up if they were down and the odds were weighed too heavily against them because, like it or not, there are times in any fight when covering up is the only option. Some of the worst damage can be sustained trying to get up off the ground during a fight because your hands are used to push you back up. You're wide open at that point so the BBC were taught that if they were down and the boots were going in they got their hands over their heads with their arms tucked in tight to protect their heads. And they only tried to get back up if the kicking had stopped. It was good, sound advice and it saved some of them from themselves because the BBC were a nutty little crew.

As they grew in strength they almost became independent of us on match days. They'd go off and fight their own battles before teaming up with us, especially on away days. Their success spawned other baby crews as well, although in nothing like the same numbers. The BBC had over a hundred guys in it at one point and, before long, other mobs were following our recruiting policy. They had baby crews of their own but more often than not they used them as spotters. They had them hang around outside pubs on match days to let them know when a rival crew was in the vicinity. Our Baby Crew was a fully fledged casual unit. They fought their battles and they fought them well. They took whatever came their way and they went back for more. They were well-trained thanks to those sessions at King's Stables Road. And they were a credit to the CCS. Why do you think we trained them in the first place?

We couldn't have them giving us a bad name.

5

PETROL BOMB ON PRINCES STREET

Seven months we had waited for this, seven long months. That was how long had passed since those miserable Aberdeen bastards kicked Raymie half to death. And now they were coming back to Edinburgh. It wouldn't have mattered if they were playing at Easter Road or Tynecastle. We'd have been there having a go. And it wouldn't have mattered if they were bringing a mob of ten or a thousand. We'd still have had a go.

In the week leading up to the game at Easter Road (on 12 October 1985) we'd shown-out big style on Princes Street. We wanted people to remember what had happened. We wanted them to join with us. We wanted to have a mob that even Aberdeen would fear and respect. And for this one the Baby Crew weren't freelancing. They were going to be with us because we needed all hands to the pump. This wasn't business. This was personal. Aberdeen had a debt to pay and by God they were going to pay it.

For all we had been showing out during the week the mood wasn't one of laughing and joking. This was no time to be messing about. We'd seen what had happened to Raymie and we'd made an arse of ourselves by going wading in at Stark's Park and getting a right doing. This time we had to be spot-on or we were finished before we'd even got properly started. A third successive hiding from Aberdeen would be the end of the CCS.

The major bright spot on the horizon was the number of people declaring themselves in for this battle. I wasn't aware that we had signed up Nutter Recruitment Inc to find us extra pairs of hands but it appeared we had. The lunatics were pitching up in their droves, telling us they'd be with our mob on the Saturday. The rest would be down to us sticking to our plans and not leaving people stranded.

We had a midweek meeting to plot the plan of action and it was agreed that on the Saturday we'd all gather in the Penny Black pub behind Burger King. It was a good place to meet up because we knew the coppers would have Waverley station surrounded. The Penny Black was handy for Princes Street but still tucked away one street back from the main drag so we were away from prying CID eyes. One of the Baby Crew would be posted on North Bridge as a lookout with another within sight of him at the junction with Princes Street. As soon as the Aberdeen mob emerged from the station we needed to know which exit they'd used, because there are three ways out of Waverley. That would tell us which route they were planning to take to the ground and where the best point to meet and greet them was.

And after the game it was agreed that we'd give it everything. Attack in battle lines, wave upon wave, and look to wear them down. See if there was any chance of mounting an ambush and catching the coppers off guard. We weren't kidding ourselves. They would have superior numbers but size isn't everything. And, as the meeting broke up that night, we agreed there was little else we could do. There was nothing for it but to wait and wonder.

The three days between that meeting and the Saturday itself felt like the longest of my life. I'm sure it was the same for the rest of the mob. All we wanted to do was to get it on and get it done and show Aberdeen their days as Scotland's number one were numbered. The seconds felt like minutes, the minutes felt like hours, the hours felt like days. But when the alarm clock finally jangled me into life on the Saturday morning, it was game on.

On match days you felt partly like one of those old generals and partly like a football coach. You wouldn't go into battle without your best dress uniform and the match-day gear had been cleaned during the week and laid out the night before. All it needed was the dressing-room peg and you were there. Then it was off to the Penny Black and the nervous wait to see what sort of mob we were going to have on the day.

It doesn't matter how many people assure you they'll turn up, you can never be certain. A guy could have gone out and got pissed the night before and wake up feeling like a fight is the last thing on his mind. Or he could have got nicked and been kept in if he was known to the coppers. Or he just might not fancy it in the cold light of day. All those factors determine the size of your mob. And all those thoughts go through your head on a match day. Can we compete? Will we have enough bodies? Will they be game boys? On this particular Saturday the answer to all three questions was a resounding yes. The Penny Black was heaving with good boys up for a bit of payback and even Raymie was there.

There's always one other subject of discussion on match day: how many of a mob you think the opposition are likely to bring. We were in no doubt Aberdeen would come down mob-handed. They knew all of Hibs were gunning for them after recent events and they'd have rounded up every man they could. That meant they'd have more bodies but, as I said, size isn't everything.

53

Even so, the sobering thought that we were once again up against it tempered any banter in the Penny Black. The general buzz was all about how we had to make a show, how we had to make a big statement on this biggest of days for us. We had to find a way of stopping them in their tracks, shaking the confidence born of arrogance that they always displayed. We had to knock their swagger into a stagger. The question was how. How on earth could we do that?

It was a throwaway line, I swear to God it was. I was even laughing as I said, 'We could always petrol-bomb the bastards.' And laughter was what that comment generated. A few of the boys echoed the comment. 'Aye, we could always petrol-bomb the bastards,' they said, as they dissolved into fits of laughter. 'Jesus Christ, Dykes,' said one of them. 'Where the fuck do you think we are? Belfast?' And he laughed even louder.

How were we to know that the Baby Crew were listening at the door of the boozer? And that there was a motorcycle parked outside the Penny Black. And that one of the BBC nipped away and found an empty bottle. And that before we'd even left the pub that day, some petrol had been siphoned off from the motorcycle's tank and run into the empty bottle, which had then been sealed at the neck with an old rag. And that the home-made Molotov cocktail had been stashed at the Penny Black. I'll swear to my dying day, none of the main men in the CCS had a clue any of that had taken place. We were just trying to stop the tears blinding us as we laughed even more at the idea of petrol-bombing the ASC.

Then we got the bad news. One of our spotters down at the station turned up to warn us that the place was crawling with coppers. They were everywhere and it was going to be a long shot to get a decent tilt at Aberdeen when they came off the train. Then we got the word they'd arrived and they'd been cute as usual. Instead of taking the shortest route out of the station – which would have meant coming straight up the stairs onto Princes Street – they had taken the ramps that let cars drive in and out of the station. If they'd used the stairs they'd have been sitting ducks, police escort or not. There were high walls on either side of those stairs and we'd have been able to launch into them from street level.

Once we knew they had a massive police escort we didn't bother charging round from the Penny Black and tearing straight into them, as we would do to several other mobs in the future. We appeared on Princes Street as they were being escorted, just to let them know we were there. They gave their '99 Soccer Reds' song big licks just to wind us up, but they would keep. There were a couple of half-hearted charges before the game from both them and us but there was no point in doing any more. If we'd gone on a full-scale charge at that point we'd have been as well cutting out the middle man and climbing straight into the back of a police van under our own steam. We'd have been nicked for certain, and unable to do anything about Aberdeen after the game, when it was bound to kick-off in earnest.

Once again, when Aberdeen were in town, the atmosphere inside Easter Road was ugly. '99 Soccer Reds' got several more airings to ensure the tension built but they thought it was great fun. They were having a right good laugh to themselves singing about kicking someone into a coma. God knows what Raymie was thinking as he listened to people joyfully singing about almost ending his life. People were up at the fence, calling them all the bastards of the day, and they were loving it. The more people had a go the louder they sang. And the more wound up we got. But do you know what the beauty of a football ground like Easter Road is? Like many of the old grounds, it's slap-bang in the middle of houses and that means that no matter how many coppers you have, there are always avenues of attack. All we had to do was to bide our time until the end of the game and we knew we'd get a shot at this mob. It turned out we were right.

After yet another depressing Hibs defeat, the coppers were clearly determined to get Aberdeen out of Edinburgh with as little trouble as possible. Now don't get me wrong, Aberdeen weren't bothering their backsides whether they had an escort or not. They were all ready to go for it as well, or at least most of them were. As they reached London Road on their way back to the station we went for it and we attacked the middle of their mob. That's where we reckoned the least-game guys normally stationed themselves and we were right on the money. Their mob split into two groups. There were about forty of us battling with the first group, who had been leading the mob up the street.

We were going at it full-on along London Road, driving them backwards towards Leith Walk, and then it really kicked off in earnest outside the Playhouse theatre. The pavement widens there and there was a lot of building work going on at the time so there was plenty of wood we could grab and use as a weapon. We still kept to our battle lines but with the coppers racing around everywhere trying to restore order there was plenty of time for scrapping. We had a full five minutes of throwing everything but the kitchen sink at each other and ninety minutes of listening to '99 Soccer Reds' had definitely given us a second wind.

They were still fighting but they were also backing off and we were now driving them up towards Princes Street and the station. They bolted down the stairs into Waverley with us at their heels and we figured they were making straight for the train. Wrong. They shot straight back up the ramp and out onto Waverley bridge, before doubling back on to Princes Street. They were obviously planning on linking up with the second group and taking on the rest of our crew mob-handed.

I had a hold of one of them and was setting about him when a hand grabbed me by the collar and the Aberdeen boy legged it. I'd been nicked and I was chucked into the back of a police van inside the station. The cop said to me, 'Where are you from?' and I replied 'Edinburgh'. 'So the other lad was Aberdeen,' he said and I nodded. 'Well,' said the copper, 'if we catch him we'll let you go.' I couldn't believe my ears. And, you know what, they nicked the fella within seconds and let me go so I was straight back into the fray.

Now, think what you like, but that convinced me the coppers were just as sickened by what had happened to Raymie as every Hibee was. I've no doubt they would deny it even now, but I think they wanted to see Aberdeen take a pounding that day. Then again, maybe they were just sick of Aberdeen coming down to Edinburgh and tearing the place up. Whatever the reason, I'm eternally grateful to him because it meant I was back on Princes Street – instead of being locked up in the back of a police van – when the defining moment in the history of the Capital City Service took place.

I'd raced up the ramp when the cops let me go and run round on to Princes Street. The second Aberdeen crew were just arriving at the station steps and that was their mob complete again, with Hibs split on either side of them. Shit! Instead of us having the upper hand, we were the mob who had been split. In the meantime, the Baby Crew boy who'd made and stashed the Molotov cocktail had slipped away unnoticed and retrieved his little present. Now bear in mind this is Saturday teatime on one of the most famous shopping thoroughfares in the world and all hell is breaking loose. There were already innocent shoppers screaming and running for cover as we charged back towards Aberdeen's crew.

Then I saw what looked like a flaming torch fly over my head towards the Aberdeen mob. All I could think was 'What the fuck' as it fizzed over my head and smashed on the ground in front of them. Then there was a kind of whoosh and the petrol caught light. If shoppers were screaming before, they were absolutely petrified now. And so were Aberdeen. They shit themselves and they turned and ran into the station. For the first time in their history, the ASC had run and it was the CCS who had made them run. Not only that, it was a fourteen-year-old Baby Crew member who had done it. Who was he? That's none of your business. Suffice to say he was never convicted and that's all you need to know.*

While Aberdeen ran in one direction, towards the train, we shot off in the other direction because we knew there would be coppers everywhere within seconds. There were but we were long gone.

Back at the Penny Black we celebrated long into the night. People who had joined up with us for the first time that day were telling us it was the most fun they'd had with their clothes on. And they had even more fun the next day when they bought their Sunday newspapers and found their Saturday-afternoon pastime was plastered all over the front page. That gave them plenty to bum about and it brought even more people into our mob.

Finally, we had arrived.

---

* Newspaper accounts confirm that the Molotov cocktail caused panic among innocent bystanders. The *Sunday Mail* of 13 October 1985 noted that 'A petrol bomber brought terror to a Scots city . . . the bomb, a lemonade bottle filled with petrol and stuffed with rags, sent people fleeing in terror when it exploded on the Waverley Steps.' AC

6

THE BIG HOOSE

The swagger that had previously belonged to Aberdeen was now ours. Every mob in the country had seen the headlines. Hibs petrol-bombed Aberdeen and the ASC ran. There was a power shift going on within the casual movement in Scotland and we were sitting at the top of the tree. It felt good, but the steep learning curve was about to come back and bite me on the backside. They say a football team is never more vulnerable than when it has just scored a goal. A casual mob was never more vulnerable than when it had just scored a success and the CCS was no different. The difference in my case was that I just didn't see it coming.

As the new number-one mob in Scotland, we were anticipating with some relish a trip to Glasgow for Hibs versus Rangers. Rangers had a pretty decent mob by then and we knew we'd be the crew they wanted to knock off their perch. That's why it was such a pain in the arse when I got lifted in 1985 before we'd even had a decent fight. Put it down to the fact I was only eighteen at the time and hadn't learned to be a bit cuter about what I was doing. We'd arrived at Glasgow's Queen Street station and were immediately corralled by the police. They were determined that if we planned to walk all the way to Ibrox, they would walk with us. We cut down through the city centre and we weren't bothered about the police being there at that point because we knew if it kicked-off it would do so in earnest about two miles away in Paisley Road West.

The whole gang was getting escorted through Central station when we spotted some of the Rangers mob hanging around in the concourse. As soon as they clocked us, one of their mob came over and started nipping away, jawing at us. I didn't want to do anything, because there were police all over us like a rash, but they were doing nothing about this joker and he was giving it big licks. Years of experience would later teach me this was normal for the Glasgow coppers. In the end up I lost it and just smacked the lippy so-and-so. It wasn't the brightest thing I ever did, considering there was a copper standing within grabbing distance. At least if I'd bided my time I might have had a chance whenever there was distance between me and the copper. Smack the boy, start running like the clappers. That would have been the smart way. But, no, I'd opted for the option marked stupid so I was nicked. And that was me, away and locked up for the weekend until I could appear at the District Court in Glasgow on the Monday morning.

Getting nicked as such didn't bother me. That part of it went with the territory and police cells aren't the worst place you'll spend a weekend. They're normally warm and clean and, unless the police station is full of headcases shouting and bawling, you can get your head down for a few hours. It's just that when you get banged up before a match on a Saturday, it's a long time until the Monday morning. That, however, generally works in your favour.

I was familiar enough with the system to know what would happen when I got to court. Normally, by the time you appear, they've had ample opportunity to check your address and you either get fined there and then or bailed to appear at a later date. For something as simple as smacking the boy in the face, I was reckoning on a fine. I'd ask for time to pay, we always did, and I'd be back in Edinburgh by the afternoon. But when I pitched up at the District Court my lawyer came to see me and dropped the bombshell. He told me they still hadn't got around to checking my address so it looked like I was going to be remanded in custody. I knew straight away what that meant. The Big Hoose.

Ask anyone in Scotland which name strikes the fear of God into them and they'll tell you: Barlinnie. It's known by many names but most folk just refer to Glasgow's notorious jail as 'The Big Hoose'. Back in the Eighties it was a place to be avoided at all costs. There had been riots, there had been prisoners on the roof hurling down slates and demonstrating about conditions inside the jail and the place was never off the telly. Every night there would be some poor reporter standing at the bottom of the driveway leading up to the jail, freezing his nuts off, telling the viewers about the latest violence taking place in the prison behind him. It was a place I had never, ever wanted to see the inside of, but now it looked as though it was exactly where I was bound for. By that stage I was shiting myself.

My lawyer reckoned there was one last card he could play to try and save my skin. He went into court and argued the case that I lived with my mother, which I did back then, and my ma stayed in Morningside. I was sitting there thinking that this guy was a genius. It sounded great: Morningside, nice address, nice part of Edinburgh. I was thinking everything should be all right because who in their right mind would send a nice lad from Morningside to The Big Hoose. I'll tell you who would. The bloody justice of the peace who was sitting on the bench in Glasgow District Court, number two, that day, that's who. 'Mr Dykes,' he said, 'we'll remand you in custody for twenty-four hours until we can get your address checked out.' I can still remember my stomach doing somersaults when he said that. So that was me. Remanded in custody. I couldn't have felt worse if he'd donned the black cap.

Did I mention I was shiting myself? Well, believe me, I was because Barlinnie was full of nutters. I was just a wee guy, a teenager, who liked a battle at the football. The lawyer came to see me and asked if there was anything he could do for me. I asked him to get me a packet of fags. He nipped round the corner from the court and brought me back cigarettes and he said he'd phone my ma to let her know what had happened. In the meantime, I was to be taken off to Barlinnie in this big prison bus. Did I mention I was shiting myself? Well I was, absolutely shiting myself, because I was the only one on that bus who had been remanded. The rest of them were off to Barlinnie to start a stretch inside.

As the bus pulled up to the prison gates I felt physically sick. It was even scarier than it looked on the telly with the big chimneys towering on top of the Victorian cell blocks. Most of the other guys on the bus weren't batting an eyelid. They'd been through all this before. I was the rookie here. When the bus went through the gates we were unloaded and marched into the reception area. I was chucked into the holding cell known as a dog box until the real nutters were processed. All I could hear were doors banging and people shouting and I was terrified. Then it was my turn to be processed. I had to give my name and address and I was on the point of losing it. I was thinking I just couldn't handle being inside Barlinnie. I've never been so scared in my life.

The one thing I was concentrating on was trying not to be cheeky to the warders because I didn't want them to throw me in a cell with some hairy-arsed rapist. Back then I didn't know that couldn't happen. Then the warders told me to empty my pockets and I did that, placing the fags the lawyer had got me on the table.

And this big warder says, 'We'll take them' and pockets the fags, with a stupid grin on his face. Bastard. I have never felt lower in my entire life than I did at that moment. Just when I thought things couldn't get any worse the fickle finger of fate gave me another poke in the balls. They'd nicked my fags as well. Everything was going through my mind. The one thought I just couldn't shake was 'I'm going to get raped in here'. And if I had been raped, I couldn't even have had a smoke afterwards!

There was another boy on remand who'd been brought in from another court and they took the two of us through the reception area into this huge main hall with cells on three levels.

Did I mention I was shiting myself? I was chalk white, shaking like a leaf. They had to take two guys out of a cell to accommodate us because young offenders don't mix with long-term prisoners. These two huge ginger-headed guys with big beards were getting turfed out of their cell for us and they were not happy. They asked us if we had any drugs but I was so scared I could barely speak.

So they left us in this cell and I was really close to tears by then. All I was thinking was to sleep with my clothes on and with my arse jammed against the wall because I was still terrified of being raped. I hardly slept a wink that night, which was no surprise really, considering I was fully clothed, with my jacket and everything still on, and my arse hard up against the wall. It wasn't a situation that lent itself to sweet dreams. God, that was a long night. Every time you'd hear a shout or a door bang you'd think this was the rape squad coming to sample some fresh meat.

I somehow made it through the night without having a nervous breakdown. In the morning the door opened and the warder told the two of us to go and get washed. With the state my mind was in by then, there was not a prayer of me having a shower. There was no way I'd spent all night protecting my arse by having it jammed against the wall to then hang it out there for the world to see in the shower room, no sir. I washed my hands and face in record time and got to fuck out of the bathrooms as quickly as I could. Then we were told to go and get some breakfast but I was stopped from doing that because I was off to court again. It wouldn't have mattered anyway. I couldn't have eaten anything.

But for the first, and last, time in my life the prospect of going to court put a spring in my step as I bounded down the stairs to get on the bus. The warders had to tell me to slow down. I was out of Barlinnie, I'd survived a night in the Bar-L; I'd made it without being raped. Let me tell you, driving away from Barlinnie is a whole lot better than driving towards it. I didn't care if they fined me a grand in court. I just didn't want to go back there.

When I got to court the lawyer came down to the cells and told me my ma and my brother were upstairs in the courtroom. Oh, I felt so happy. And when I got into the court I could see them sitting there and one of my mates had come through from Edinburgh as well. I was nearly in tears because all I wanted was a cuddle from my ma. Tough guy, eh? Thankfully, I got bail at the second attempt. I walked out of the court straight towards my ma, arms outstretched, looking for my cuddle. And she just whacked me straight across the face, a sore one too. 'Ya bloody arsehole,' she said, but I was happy to take that just to go home.

We got on the train, me with the fingerprint mark still on my face, trailing along behind her like a two-year-old. They let me on to the carriage first and I sat down at a table of four. The other three sat down, then got up and walked away and sat down at another table. 'You're stinking,' they said. 'We're not sitting next to you all the way through to Edinburgh. Couldn't you have had a wash?' If only they'd known what I'd been through but my ma was so mad with me there was no point in telling her.

And you know what? I didn't care; I was out of the Bar-L and I was going home. As I sat on that train I swore to myself I was finished with the Capital City Service and battling because the whole experience had been so terrifying. I think my ma thought that would be me finished as well and secretly she'd have been delighted I'd had the scare I needed. But no sooner was I back home than I got a call from one of my mates. We arranged to meet that night and my plan was to tell them how I had been shiting myself. But it never quite works like that, does it?

You have to realise that this was a big event for everybody: one of the crew had got remanded and put in the Bar-L. And when the boys are asking for tales about what it was like inside The Big Hoose, you're not going to tell them you were like a scared wee boy. No, no, no. The chest was puffed out, the story grew arms and legs as the night went on and, before you knew it, I had that wee bit extra respect from the rest of the crew. You're telling them, 'Nah, the Bar-L never bothered me. Piece of piss.'

Oh, but it fucking did. By God it did.

7

SLASHED AND BURNED

The petrol-bombing of Aberdeen had taken things to a new level between the two mobs. The one thing it had proved for certain was that we would stop at nothing to retain our position as Scotland's top mob. We knew that would be sorely tested when we travelled north to Pittodrie to face them on their patch in 1987. They were still seething about the petrol bomb, they'd made that clear over the phone. The fact we'd also fired a distress flare at them during a subsequent battle in Princes Street had merely cranked up the animosity. It sounds dangerous but all it did was hit one of their boys on the leg and knock him off his feet. We weren't firing it at head height but I can understand why they'd be so pissed off. But that was how we felt about them back then. Serious injury was always a risk for them, but they had started it with the Raymie incident.

For the trip to Aberdeen in 1987 we decided not to risk going by train. For one thing, there was a chance we could be ambushed at the station. There was also the problem of coppers escorting us straight from the station to the ground, which would leave us with no room for manoeuvre. Taking all this into account, we hired two buses and left early in the morning so that we'd be in Aberdeen before their mob had tumbled to the fact we'd arrived.

The first plan of the plan went exactly as we'd hoped. We arrived in Aberdeen without any problems, got the bus drivers to drop us off miles away from the ground and found a pub well off the main drag to have a couple of beers. There was always something about facing Aberdeen which was different from facing any other mob. Even as we were sitting back enjoying a pint, and on the face of it everyone appeared relaxed, you knew that inside they weren't. The chatter was always a little more manic, the laughter a little more forced, the eyes always darting this way and that. The guys were tense, but that was no sign of weakness, more of readiness. Battles with Aberdeen were always brutal and you had to feel nervous about what lay ahead, especially in unfamiliar surroundings.

But as two o'clock came it was time to move. We made our way through the streets, knowing the chances of an ambush were now slim. They'd be ensconced in their pub, the Premier Bar, right across the road from the Beach End at Pittodrie. If you're not familiar with Pittodrie it's one of the coldest places on God's earth because it's right next to the North Sea. And as you make your way to that ground, the wind blowing off the sea chills you to the marrow. You climb up a grassy hill and, when you get to the top, the ground's right there in front of you across the road. Then you make your way down the other side of the hill and you're at the Premier Bar. That bar was ideal for Aberdeen's mob because any rival mobs making their way to the ground could be seen as soon as they breasted the rise on the hill. They always had spotters outside so they were ready and waiting by the time the rival mob reached the pub car park.

Nothing had changed that day. We were atop the hill, a couple of young boys shot straight into the boozer to raise the alarm, and by the time Aberdeen emerged we were charging down the hill like extras in *Braveheart*. They were ready for us and we were more than ready for them. We didn't even break stride as we barrelled our way into the car park and past their first wave. I could see their top boy off to my left and there was hatred in his eyes, pure hatred. But I had my hands full with the guy in front of me and I caught him a dull one to the face. It dazed him and I thumped him again and got a hold of the back of his jacket. I had both hands on his back and was pushing him downwards while I stuck the boot into him. He was groaning when the boots landed but then he let out a yelp, and so did I. The adrenaline normally numbs the pain but not when you've just been slashed across the back of the hand. And it hurts even more when it's one of your own mob who's done you.

As I was holding the Aberdeen boy down and booting into him, one of our guys had pulled out a Stanley knife and gone to slash his neck. He succeeded, but not before the blade had sliced across the back of my hand first. If it had been my right hand it wouldn't have been so bad. But as a kid I'd spilled boiling water on the back of my left hand and badly damaged the skin. It was paper thin and the Stanley blade had done some serious damage.

I still had my hands on the boy's back and as I looked down at it I was seeing bones and tendons and bits of my hand I really didn't want to see. The Aberdeen boy, meanwhile, had blood running down the back of his neck, some of it his, some of it mine.

The coppers arrived to break up the fight within seconds of the slashing and as they separated the two mobs I was standing with one hand holding the other upright to try and stem the flow of blood. They soon spotted me and took me away from the mobs and into a bus shelter while they radioed for an ambulance. I looked across at my brother and he was chalk white because he could see the blood running down my arm. It was a bad one all right, and with the adrenaline no longer pumping, it was sheer agony. The coppers did their best to wrap up my hand while we waited for the ambulance but it was taking forever.

The two mobs had been herded off to their respective ends of the ground by then and the game was under way but I was still stuck in this bus shelter waiting for the ambulance to arrive. In the end it never did. The cops got sick of waiting and took me to hospital in their squad car, which I very ungratefully bled all over. While I was sitting with the two cops waiting to see a doctor, they kept getting messages on their radios and they'd wander off to talk to their boss, or whoever was calling them. I didn't know what they were being told but they informed me that whenever I was patched up I'd be coming to the station with them. I figured I was going to get done for giving the boy a kicking. I'd heard the Aberdeen cops were clamping down hard on their mob and this was the first taste of it I'd experienced.

When I finally got taken through to a cubicle a nurse came and took a look at me but said they'd need to get a doctor to examine the injury because it was so serious. The cops weren't too chuffed with that, because it meant more hanging around the hospital. Me? I wasn't bothered. I just wanted my hand to be better and lying on a bed in accident and emergency beat sitting in a cell in some police station. The doctor eventually came and poked and prodded and did what doctors do. Then he announced I would need surgery because a couple of tendons had been severed. I would have to stay in hospital. Now that was a real result. The cops went off to get a cup of tea and await further instructions from their boss about what they should do.

In my position most folk would have lain back on the bed, relaxed, and waited for whatever surgery was required. And that would have been the sensible thing. Not me. I had a plan to get out of there, leg it back to Edinburgh and dodge any charge that might be coming my way. I called the nurse over and asked her if there was any way I could just be patched up and have the surgery done when I got home. She wasn't having that; she looked at me as though I had a screw loose. But I told her straight that I was signing myself out, whether she patched me up or not, and she reluctantly agreed. She wanted to go and get the coppers but I told her I'd be gone by the time she came back if she did that. I assured her that if I got caught I'd say I nicked the bandage and not drop her in it. So she wrapped this huge bandage around my injured hand. I looked as though I had nicked a limb from the mummy but, after checking the coast was clear, I sneaked away.

I got outside the hospital no problem and hailed the first taxi I saw. This was going brilliantly. I told the driver to head for the centre of Aberdeen, but to keep driving until I told him to stop. There it was, just what I was looking for. The Aberdeen-to-Edinburgh bus. I paid off the taxi driver, ran across Union Street in front of the bus and got the driver's attention, just as he was about to move off. I almost jumped the steps into the bus in one go and asked, 'How much is it to Edinburgh, mate?' 'I could tell you,' he said, 'but it won't do you any good. I've just come from Edinburgh. This bus terminates at the garage.' What an arsehole I was. I'd got on a bus on the wrong side of the street. I had no choice but to get off the bus because it was going nowhere I wanted to go.

By this time it was knocking on seven o'clock and being stuck on Union Street wasn't an option. For one thing, it was where a lot of their mob hung around at night. If I got spotted here, flying solo, a damaged hand would be the least of my worries. Considering one of their boys had been slashed that afternoon, I'd be the revenge for him and that prospect didn't appeal. At the same time the cops would also be looking for me since I'd done a runner from the hospital. I wasn't too keen on being banged up for the weekend either but going to the cops was the lesser of two evils. The sort of banged up Aberdeen's mob would dish out would be far worse. So that was it settled then, the fugitive would turn himself in. I headed for the nearest cop shop because at least it meant I'd be off Union Street and the cops wouldn't give me a kicking.

As I wandered into the police station there were two Hibs scarfers there. Their brother had been nicked at the game and they were waiting to see if they could get him out before heading home. I sat down to have a chat with them and get the low-down on the game. They told me I hadn't missed much and asked what had happened to my hand. I passed it off as being jumped by a bunch of Aberdeen. If I'd told them what had really happened they'd have run a mile. Just then the desk sergeant came out and announced there was no chance of their brother being released that night, so they got up to go. 'Hang on, boys,' I said, 'do you have a car?' They told me they did, it was parked right outside; I asked if there was chance of a lift back to Edinburgh. They had no problems with that so the great escape was back on.

It was a smashing journey back down the road. All we talked was football, football, football, reminiscing about the great Hibs games and goals and bemoaning the lack of success of recent seasons. I was getting on famously with these two lads and, as we approached Dundee, I was figuring it would only take us another hour or so to reach Edinburgh. I'd told these boys to drop me off in Edinburgh wherever it suited them and I'd make my way home from there. Getting a taxi across Edinburgh would be a small price to pay for dodging the coppers and the ASC.

But just as I was dreaming of getting home, there was the wailing of a siren and flashing blue lights behind us. The cop car flashed our car to stop. I joked with our driver and said, 'I hope you were keeping to the speed limit there. The cops up here are bastards for dishing out speeding fines.' The driver got out and spoke to the cops and the conversation lasted a good few minutes. I couldn't work out what was going on until the driver came back and said to me, 'It's you they want to talk to.' I clambered out of the passenger seat and the cops asked me my name. Once I'd confirmed it they said, 'You're coming with us.'

'Where to?' I asked. 'Aberdeen,' came the reply.

I couldn't believe it. I'd been an hour from Edinburgh and now I was going all the way back to Aberdeen. To me this seemed like overkill for a bit of a punch-up before a football game, especially when I'd been the most seriously injured party in that punch-up. Because I was so pissed off at being hauled all the way back up to Aberdeen I mentioned that to the cops. Then they dropped the bombshell. The punch-up didn't bother them. It had been alleged that it was me who slashed the boy. Now, by any stretch of the imagination, that was pushing it. Were they really saying that I accidentally slashed my own hand while slashing somebody else? It was ridiculous. But that was what the cops were telling me was being claimed, so I'd have to go back to Aberdeen to face the music.

On the journey back I also asked them how they'd known where to find me. It turned out there was closed-circuit television monitoring the front of the cop shop, where the boys' car had been parked. Once I'd legged it from the hospital the word had gone round the cops to keep an eye out for me. They had a description of what I was wearing and they thought my hand would be bandaged. That was the giveaway. The desk sergeant had recognised the description and I hadn't even bothered trying to hide my bandaged hand because I was going there to give myself up until I got the chance of the lift. I could have saved myself hours of travelling between Aberdeen and Dundee by just going straight to the cop shop in the first place. What a bloody miserable turn of events.

It wasn't to get much better either. When I got back to Aberdeen they told me I'd be kept in a cell for the weekend to appear in court on the Monday morning. I chanced my arm and told them I needed an operation on my hand. It was pure cheek but I told them I had to go back to hospital. Surprisingly, they agreed and a bed was found for me in the hospital. On Monday morning, surgeons repaired the two damaged tendons and stitched up the wound to the back of my hand and I was discharged the next day.

Even then, I couldn't get out of Aberdeen. I had a court date that afternoon. I met with my lawyer and he told me I was being charged with slashing the boy with a broken beer glass. He said I would be best to plead guilty and I exploded. Why on earth would I plead guilty to something I didn't do? What about the slash wound across the back of my hand? Then my lawyer told me the police had ten statements from the Aberdeen mob, in which they swore they had seen me slash their boy. The statements claimed I'd hit him with a beer glass which then smashed and, when it did so, a large piece of glass had cut me across the back of the hand. It was Jackanory time. A Stanley blade makes a clean cut. Broken glass makes a jagged cut. It was nonsense.

But there had been an outcry in the Aberdeen papers about another outbreak of casual violence and the fact someone got slashed merely upped the ante. People wanted action and it seemed I was the fall guy to reassure the Aberdeen public that the police were on top of it. And, of course, it gave the Aberdeen mob a way of getting back at the CCS by getting one of us done for slashing their boy, even if they were lying through their teeth.

The lawyer told me that if I pleaded not guilty in the face of ten witness statements, the court would hammer me if I was found guilty. I had no choice; I stood there and pleaded guilty to something I didn't do. They fined me £250 and, at last, I could leave

Aberdeen. It had taken two police cars, a bus, a private car, a taxi, and finally a train. But I was on my way home.

When I got home the phone rang. It was the boy who'd slashed me and he wasn't sure what to say. 'Is your hand OK?' he asked. 'Aye,' I said. 'Did you tell them it was me who did the slashing?' he said. 'What do you think?' I replied. 'Thanks mate,' he said.

Well, that's what being part of a mob is all about.

8

ONE AFTERNOON IN GOVAN

Ever since I'd got banged up in Barlinnie in 1985 I'd despised the Rangers mob. Rightly or wrongly, I blamed them for putting me through hell that weekend because they'd sent one wee ned to start chipping at us at the railway station. Hibs didn't like Rangers much anyway. There had been battles between fans of the clubs for years before we arrived on the scene, most of it down to misperceptions on the part of Rangers fans about Hibs' Irish heritage. And, by the late Eighties, the fact that both teams had decent crews meant every game between the sides was a flashpoint.

We knew in advance what we were getting into when we went to Glasgow. There would be a battle with their mob, with their scarfers very keen to pitch in and lend a hand. We also knew that the Glasgow police would be only too happy to stand with their hands folded behind their backs and refuse to intervene if the battle was going Rangers' way. If it wasn't, they'd be in like a shot and nick the lot of us. When you went to Glasgow, you were up against more than just the opposition mob. The Rangers mob called itself the ICF, the Inter City Firm, not exactly stunningly original. It was the name that had already been adopted by West Ham and there was a supposed link between the firms.

But we were always up for a trip to Glasgow because there was something extra special about walking Scotland's largest city. Walking was what casuals did. You didn't take public transport to whatever ground you were headed for. You walked. It was a way of telling the opposition mob you had no fear of them, or their scarfers, or anyone else who wanted to stick their oar in. It didn't matter whether the ground was one mile away or five miles away. We always walked in Glasgow. I don't think I even realised you could get a tube to Ibrox until many years later. Because we walked, we were guaranteed a battle because you were alongside Rangers on the way there, and again on the way back.

The plan for our visit to Ibrox in eighty-seven was simple. We'd meet in Waverley station itself for this one. There was no point in congregating somewhere else beforehand because a two-hundred-strong mob descending on the station as one group would stick out like a sore thumb. If we did that the Edinburgh coppers would be on to their Glasgow colleagues in a heartbeat and there would van-loads of police waiting for us in Glasgow. We all knew the train we were planning to catch so it was simply a case of arriving as late as possible so we weren't kept hanging around in the station and drawing attention to ourselves.

We caught our train to Queen Street station in Glasgow and there wasn't a lot of conversation on the way. There was always tension in the air on the way to Glasgow because you knew their mob would be tooled up. They always were and it was almost as if you were playing Russian roulette through there. You might avoid getting cut the first or second time but the likelihood was they would get you in the end. You never knew if this was the time that you were going to get stabbed. Once we got to Queen Street it wasn't rocket science. We walked. You never had to worry about an ambush at the station from Rangers. They were content to sit in their own patch and let you come to them. That was fine by us. It wasn't as if we didn't know where to find them. It also saved us from getting nicked before we got there.

So we came out of the station, headed down Buchanan Street, cut along Argyle Street, over the Jamaica Street bridge and turned right; about half a mile from there is the start of Paisley Road West. There is a wee pub that sits directly beneath the Kingston bridge at the start of Paisley Road West. That was where the first fight kicked off. Rangers had sent an advance party to test our bottle and they got the shock of their lives. I don't think they expected us to be as mob-handed as we were and they were seen off with no trouble. For us, it was the ideal starter course. It got the blood pumping and now we were really up for it.

It wouldn't have made any difference if we weren't because once you were on Paisley Road West that was you. There was nowhere else to go, at least nowhere we knew about. That area wasn't easy to recce because it was so solidly Rangers. Sending a scout to take a look in advance would have been sending a guy for a certain kicking. We weren't bothered anyway. This was what we had come for: to show Rangers on their own patch just who was the number-one crew.

We already had our battle lines set up and there was a group of twenty people in front of everyone else. They were the complete loonies and they would start everything. They could hold their own and everyone else would have to catch up with them. I was in that group and as we reached Paisley Road Toll there was another mob of Rangers waiting. Our little group battled its way straight through them and left the rest of the CCS to deal with them in the time-honoured fashion – with a right good kicking.

We were more interested in getting the main event underway and we had little further to go for that. We were headed for the District Bar. It's a pub that sits on Paisley Road West just beyond where the road narrows. There are two pubs just before that on either side of the road. They deal with the overspill from the District Bar on match days so that particular area wasn't for the faint hearted. There was always a Rangers mob there, predictably backed up by a healthy contingent of scarfers. And we were off and running. There was no point in giving it the casual swagger because they'd have got the shout from down the road that we were arriving in a hurry. They were waiting for us but we didn't miss a beat. We steamed straight into them, confident the cavalry, in the shape of the rest of our mob, would soon be arriving to even up the numbers.

The fight spilled from the pavement into the middle of the road and that's a dangerous game. Paisley Road West is no Glasgow back street; it's one of the main routes into the city centre. You had as much chance of getting mown down by a passing car or bus as you did of getting dropped by a punch or a kick. Have you any idea how tough it is to fight when you're keeping one eye on the people in front of you and the other on the traffic that is honking horns and swerving to avoid you? Now that's multi-tasking. And part of that multi-tasking is keeping an eye out for the rest of your crew.

About a hundred of us were involved in the battle by this time but I didn't realise the rest of our mob were still battling further down the road. The lead group had pushed too far ahead and moved too quickly and that meant our mob was split. It just shows you, it doesn't matter how much you plan, mayhem still happens. Once the adrenaline is pumping, strategies go out of the window. But at that time we had some decent, decent guys in our crew. Every single one of them was up for a fight. They didn't run, no matter what was happening around them.

It wasn't like when we started out and everyone was in love

with the idea of being a casual and not knowing what that meant. These guys were only coming with the mob to fight. They knew exactly what was expected of them and they would never run. They weren't coming along thinking, 'We might get a fight here.' Their attitude could be summed up in two words: I'm in. The whole attitude had changed. And because these guys were so good and so committed it didn't matter that the mob had been split. The rear half eventually won their battle, we did our bit up front and there was no way the Rangers mob were up for having at a go at our second wave as they charged through. They were content to regroup and wait until after the match.

We marched the rest of the way to Ibrox with an extra swagger. We'd done Rangers on their own patch and we still had the entire mob intact. We'd done them so quickly and so efficiently that the police didn't have a chance to get involved. The coppers didn't look overly chuffed when we swanned up to Ibrox, two-hundred-strong, and marched along Edmiston Drive in front of the main stand to get to the visiting end. There were the usual taunts from the Rangers cavemen who hung around outside the main entrance to the ground but we could afford to ignore them. Their mates would have been telling them how we were going to be annihilated in Paisley Road West yet here we were, large as life. They'd find out who'd got annihilated when their mates turned up.

Inside the ground, it was like any other match involving Rangers. There was just wall-to-wall hate raining down on the small band of Hibs fans, mixed in with a hefty dollop of Loyalist songs. But as were watching Hibs lose, which wasn't unusual at Ibrox back then, we had more to concern us. You never normally plan your route away from a stadium because the coppers generally take care of that for you. A hefty police escort is the norm, especially when the visiting mob numbers two hundred. But on this occasion we were torn between going along with the escort, or going back for another go at Rangers. We'd damaged them on the way into Ibrox; we could do more damage on the way back. In the end we decided on the latter option. We'd go back for round two.

Again we had to be cute. The moment we got up out of our seats to leave the stadium all police leave would be cancelled. There would be a reception committee waiting right outside the exit for us. We left in ones and twos about ten minutes before the final whistle, the plan being to turn the opposite way when we left the ground. Instead of turning left when we reached Edmiston Drive, and going along the front of the main stand towards Paisley Road West, we turned right. That took us towards a roundabout and the street that goes down towards Govan from there was where the Hibs supporters buses were parked. The cops didn't give us a second look as we headed that way. They probably figured we'd had enough of seeing Hibs being beaten.

Once we got to the supporters buses we simply waited until the whole mob had turned up. Then we walked down by the Albion Way pub and tried to get our bearings. Ibrox stadium itself helped because it towers over everything else in the area. We knew that as long as we kept it on our right, then behind us, we'd be heading in the right direction. And, lo and behold, after twenty-five minutes of wandering through some pretty crummy parts of Glasgow we looked up a side street. There, on the corner, was the District Bar.

We knew the Rangers mob would be ensconced by then, with their spotters further up Paisley Road West, waiting for a sight of the police escort bringing us along the street. We picked up a heavy litter bin and carted it straight through the side window. Then we tanned the window next to that and we wound up putting in all their windows. That got their attention. They came out of the place growling but we were more than ready to take them on.

The only problem was, as we were squaring up to them, Paisley Road West was wall-to-wall with Rangers fans making their way back into town. The CCS against the Rangers crew would have been a fair fight but now they had thousands upon thousands of scarfers to back them up. Well, we'd picked the fight so there was nothing to do but get on with it. It was a battle and a half. There was surge and counter surge with them thirsting for revenge and us using every ounce of energy we had. We were doing some serious damage to them but, believe me, they were doing some serious damage to us as well.

In a situation like that you always figure the coppers will get there before people get seriously butchered but, to be fair to them, they simply couldn't get through to stop the fight. The road was completely clogged up with fans making their way back from Ibrox and their only way to get to the scene was to come through those thousands of fans. The fans weren't about to move out of the way, not when they had two hundred Hibs cornered.

The battle must have lasted ten or fifteen minutes and it was superb. Rangers were ripping up paving stones and launching them at us. I got hit in the chest and shoulder with paving stones but when the adrenaline is pumping you don't feel any pain. It was only once the coppers finally got to the scene and broke up the fight that I realised I had been slashed three times down my right side. There were three big slash marks in my jacket but, as I said, you don't really feel any pain when you're fighting. You're too focused on staying upright, on not going down and becoming a sitting duck.

As more and more coppers arrived Paisley Road West was closed off. A load of our boys had got off their marks when the coppers arrived, which was fair enough. The police marched the seventy-two of our mob who were left on to the other side of the road and lined us up against the wall outside a wee Post Office. The Rangers mob were kept on the other side and there were lines of coppers standing in the middle of the road, keeping us apart. Then a whole fleet of police vans arrived, obviously to lift everyone and take them off to the cells.

I thought I'd pull a fast one and I let myself slide on to the pavement as if I had collapsed. I was confident they would buy it because I had the slash marks and there was blood oozing out from my shirt. A copper knelt over me to see what was wrong and, just to add a convincing touch, I mumbled that I'd been hit in the chest with a paving stone. All I wanted was for them to take me to hospital because I was sure it would save me from getting nicked. The plan was working a treat. The copper radioed for an ambulance to come to the scene and it arrived, siren blaring, to whisk me off to the Southern General hospital.

To be fair, it wasn't as much of an act as I first thought. They took a fair bit of time cleaning up my slash wounds and while my chest wasn't really injured, they put my arm in a sling because of the blow I'd taken to the shoulder with the other cobblestone. I was sitting there being treated, thinking I'd pulled a real fast one on the coppers. At that point, I was fancying my chances of getting back to Queen Street station, getting the train back to Edinburgh and catching last orders on home territory. But as I walked out of the accident-and-emergency area at the hospital, there were two of Strathclyde's finest waiting on me. The first of them put it in plain and simple terms. 'Right Mr Dykes, you're coming with us.' Shit, shit, shit. Before I knew it I was being taken away to Govan police station, because that was where they had the rest of the boys.

But once I got inside the station it was hilarious. I had come up the stairs and I walked in past the holding cells. One of my mates heard my voice as I was talking to the coppers and he yelled out 'Dykes, ya fucking arsehole.' Before long the word had gone round the various cells that I was okay. Next thing the CCS songs were being sung, the windows were being battered and boys were raising merry hell. How touching. They were worried about me.

It didn't last long. The next thing they were giving me dog's abuse for pulling the dying-swan act. They were just raging they hadn't thought of it themselves. Or maybe they had, and I'd got in first. But as they were calling me all the chancers of the day, the copper on the desk told me I would have the last laugh. They had no more room in the cells because so many Hibs and Rangers had been lifted. I was the last of us to be processed and that made it seventy-two Hibs in all. So I was only getting my fingerprints taken, being photographed and being signed out to appear in court at a later date.

As I was walking back past the holding cells I said: 'See you later boys' and they were going mental. I caught the train and also caught last orders in Edinburgh while the rest of them were banged up overnight. Two battles in one day with Rangers and home before shutting time.

Now that was a Saturday to remember.

* * *

If you ever wanted proof that all the planning in the world can't stop things going wrong, it came in 1988 when we went to Ibrox.

We had something really special in mind for that day because Rangers were still making noises about being the best. We were determined to show them once and for all that when it came to putting on a show on another mob's patch, we were the top men. This one had taken a lot of planning and had been weeks in the preparation. Ibrox was the ground where it would work perfectly and, of course, there was the small matter of showing Rangers who was boss.

The subject had first been raised during a meeting of our gang of five. We were planning a ruck at a home game when the subject of the battle of Paisley Road West was brought up. At that time, it had been our greatest battle and one we all remembered with great pride. And, as we reminisced, someone suggested we should try and top it the next time we visited Ibrox. We debated going into their end but it wasn't really on at Ibrox. They had so many fans you couldn't get in there. Hibs were given a bit in the main stand. Going into their end and kicking off was a non-starter and, as we knocked ideas around, someone said, 'We need to get some real fireworks going.' That was it. We'd fired a flare at Aberdeen in Princes Street before. Why not fire one at Rangers. But instead of doing it in Paisley Road West, we'd do it inside Ibrox. That would set down a real marker for every other mob.

Getting the flare wouldn't be a problem. We had a contact down at Leith docks who could get us flares any time we wanted. These weren't the little flares some mobs used, particularly Celtic and Rangers. Their two mobs fired little flares about the size of a large marker pen and they were a pain in the arse. I lost count of the number of jackets I had ruined with those things because when they hit your jacket they burned it and left a scorch mark. A bloody nuisance was what they were. But we weren't playing around with mini-flares. Our boy in the docks could get us the real thing: great big distress flares. And if we were going to put on a firework display, we'd be as well making sure the fireworks went with a bang. We'd also take a smoke bomb and thunder-flash along with us. That would give Rangers something to think about.

First off, we had to check out their ground. That was risky and could result in a kicking, but we took a chance and went through to Glasgow one midweek when they were playing. Obviously we'd been to Ibrox plenty of times before but we had to know how easy it was going to be to get the stuff in. We had a look at the people going through the turnstiles and noticed that the fans going into the stands behind the goals were being searched. The people going into the main stand weren't, presumably because they were the posh folk; funny how the scruff always gets the wrong end of the deal. But that was perfect for us. If we could get tickets for the main stand, towards the Broomloan Road end, we'd be sitting directly above their mob. We knew their mob went into the enclosure at that end so it would be ideal to be right above them. The plan was in operation.

Over the next few weeks we contacted our guy at Leith docks, placed our order for the flare and sorted out the supply of the smoke bomb and thunder-flash. Then it was about the route. The problem with toting that lot through to Ibrox was that someone would have to carry it, and that meant bringing a bag. You couldn't scrap with a rucksack on your back so you'd be there for the taking by Rangers. And getting off the train amongst our mob carrying a rucksack was a sure-fire way of attracting the coppers. We thought about going by bus but that would have the coppers sniffing about as well. They'd wonder what the hell was going on if we didn't do our usual and come through on the train. Coppers don't like change.

So, albeit reluctantly, we settled on doing the things the way we'd always done them. A bunch of us would go through to Glasgow in the week before the game and buy tickets for the main stand. One guy with an Edinburgh accent buying fifty might have attracted attention. So that was that, all set.

There was just one other issue to deal with. We'd have to talk to the boys in advance of this one, because we needed a volunteer to carry the rucksack and let off the flare and the other pyrotechnics inside Ibrox. The rucksack was the biggest issue because we couldn't afford to have one of our really game boys carry it. On the day we'd still need to battle our way up Paisley Road West to get to Ibrox and that normally meant all hands to the pump in the scrapping department. In the end one wee guy volunteered, not only to carry the rucksack, but also to set off the flare, and he assured us he knew what he was doing.

Come the day of the game we were like school kids. That's what it was like, a school outing. Everyone was excited and we'd gone the whole hog by donning Peter Storm jackets and National Health specs. I don't know what we thought we were doing, we stood out like a sore thumb. And this on a day when the main object of the exercise wasn't battling on the way to the game but getting to the stadium in one piece with the bag intact.

But the get-up worked a treat. We caught the train through to Glasgow and the coppers at Queen Street were so taken aback by the get-up I don't think they even noticed the boy with the bag. We walked down Buchanan Street, mob-handed, not giving a toss about anyone. There was a load of Rangers scarfers going into the subway station at St Enoch Square as we reached the bottom of Buchanan Street and they drew us the usual look but settled for giving it verbals from a distance. They weren't about to risk coming any closer than the hundred yards or so they had for protection.

The excitement levels were building but we couldn't afford to take our eye off the ball. Paisley Road West was looming and we knew what was coming there. The Rangers mob and their cavemen would be forming their usual guard of dishonour and we'd have to fight our way through it. It's Sod's Law, of course. On the day you just want the easiest possible walk up to Ibrox, they've got twice as many as they would normally have.

By the time we reached Paisley Road Toll, our mob had been split. The Glasgow coppers were doing their usual, keeping a discreet distance and waiting to see Hibs get a hiding. Once again, they were disappointed because the first group battled their way through and headed on towards the District Bar, leaving our second group to tidy up behind us. And as we were heading up the road, the spotters disappeared inside the pub and their mob were out and waiting. We had to make this quick because we needed to get the boy with the bag through without the coppers taking a look. He was with us in the front group so we were also relying on the second group to catch up quickly and give us a hand. We steamed into Rangers and were reassured to see the second group coming battering up the road at full tilt to get stuck in as well. The boy with the bag was shoved off to one side and told to keep out of trouble while we got stuck in.

But any hopes we had of making it easy were scuppered when some nutter appeared brandishing a machete. He was roaring like a bull and screaming 'Come on ya bastards' and swinging this big blade around. Christ, this was a bit more serious than some prick with a Stanley knife. And there were coppers standing watching this. The headcase with the machete started chasing Jed, one of our boys. The two of them were either side of a parked car and the nutter was trying to close the gap on Jed. They were running round and round the car and it was like a cartoon. It would have been funny, apart from the fact that this guy had a machete.

Still the coppers stood idly by and didn't intervene. They only stepped in to grab the headcase once he'd caught up with Jed, whacked him with the machete, and split his head open. The cops radioed for an ambulance so we all had to wait while Jed was treated and taken away to hospital. Despite that, there was still no full-scale police escort to Ibrox. Maybe they were hoping we'd get a doing before we got there. The bright mood had darkened a little with the injury to Jed. He was a good boy, one of the really game ones, and it was a nightmare to see him get injured like that. But we all popped the daft NHS specs back on and started acting like idiots and the laughter was back. Getting taken out when you're on the road could happen to anyone.

By the time we reached Ibrox we were at fever pitch. We had to calm ourselves down to stop the stewards getting suspicious. The only guy who wasn't excited was the wee bloke with the bag. He looked pale and sweaty. He was shiting himself. Whether he thought the whole plan was just too far-fetched and would never happen, I don't know. But now he was standing outside Ibrox, seconds away from trying to enter a football ground with a bag containing a smoke bomb, a thunder-flash and a flare. What's your defence if you get caught with those? You were going to a rock concert on a boat?

We joined the small queue of people waiting to go into the main stand and shoved the wee guy to the front. He handed over his ticket, the steward looked at the rucksack on his back and we thought the game was up. And then he waved him through. Didn't open the bag, or even pat it. Nothing. You beauty. The rest of us followed one by one and took our seats and they were exactly where we wanted. Right above the Rangers mob. Oh, this was going to be some day.

The only dark cloud on our horizon was our wee guy. If he'd been pale and sweaty before he looked positively drained now. The stress of getting through the turnstile unchecked had been too much for him. He took the rucksack off and placed it at his feet and looked at it as though there was a time bomb in it. We tried our best to calm him down but his mind was gone. We just had to hope he'd be okay by the time we wanted him to set off the flare.

The plan was to toss the smoke bomb and thunder-flash into their mob beneath us, then fire the flare across at the stand directly opposite the main stand. The wee guy had assured us he knew what he was doing with the flare and we had to take his word for it.

The whole thing was going to take place twenty minutes into

the game and we knew the rest of our mob would have set their watches for the big event.

Once the match was twenty minutes old we got the stuff out of the bag and told the wee guy to get ready with the flare. He just shook his head and mumbled that he wasn't doing it. 'Just fucking do it,' he was told and he nodded. One of our boys tossed the thunder-flash and the smoke bomb over the front of the stand into the terracing below. Nothing. Not a thing. Neither of them went off. We'd been sold a pair of duds. And the wee guy's still humming and hawing about the flare. 'Fucking do it or we'll fucking do you.'

So he did it.

You know that moment in the Michael Douglas film *Falling Down* where he's got the rocket launcher? And he doesn't know how to use it but a wee boy shows him. And he presses the trigger and it turns out he's holding the rocket launcher back to front and the rocket shoots out behind him and nearly blows a road gang to kingdom come. We knew how he felt that day. Instead of firing the flare across at the other stand, our wee guy fired it vertically. It shot straight up into the metal framework of the stand roof above our heads, went off and showered us all in red-hot sparks. The big cheer we expected from the rest of our mob was a groan. Then the bloody flare dropped out of the metal framework and in among us. We were hopping about like idiots, trying to avoid being torched by our own flare.

What a bloody disaster. You lose one of your good guys with a machete wound to the back of the head, throw two dud devices at the opposition which would only be good for giving them a nasty bump on the head, then damn-near incinerate yourself with your own flare. Once the thing had stopped burning there was nothing else for it. We sat and watched the game. Guess what? Hibs lost 1–0. And the wee guy who set off the flare got nicked at the ground after they checked the closed-circuit television.

Now that's what you call a bad day at the office.

* * *

Believe me, it wasn't the worst day I've had at Ibrox. A year later we were leaving the ground after a game and we had a police escort. Rangers were on one side of the road; we were on the other. I was walking beside my mate Ross when the charge started from their side just at the roundabout outside Ibrox. Someone reached around from behind us and cut Ross on the back of the neck with a Stanley knife. I sat him down by a wall and waited with him for the ambulance to come but the rest of our boys had been moved on by the police.

There were two coppers waiting with us to make sure none of their mob came back and took liberties. Then, when Ross had been loaded into the ambulance, the two coppers got a hold of me and told me I was being charged with slashing him. I just laughed at them. What, I slashed the bloke I was walking along the road with? But they charged me and locked me up and I had to appear in court.

Ross came through from Edinburgh and gave evidence on my behalf saying it was ridiculous I'd been charged because he'd been hit from behind and I was alongside him. He also knew I would have been unarmed because I didn't carry blades to the football. My lawyer was certain his evidence would get me off. But the judge preferred the evidence of two cops who said they had witnessed me doing it, which was a total lie. My lawyer was amazed at the verdict, totally astonished. But I got fined, I can't even remember how much.

And you wonder why I don't like Glasgow cops?

9

CELTIC LEARNED THE HARD WAY

By the mid 1980s it was rare indeed for a mob other than Hibs to command the headlines for events that took place in and around Easter Road. But Celtic, an utterly ineffective mob, managed it on 28 November 1987. The preamble to the match had been unremarkable. The Celtic crew had arrived on buses and concealed themselves among their scarfers as they always did on those occasions. Celtic's support were different from the norm because they never, ever embraced the casual culture. Even at their home ground, Parkhead, Celtic's crew got a hard time from their fellow fans.

We'd experienced that at the outset at Easter Road but over time the Hibs scarfers, while not necessarily approving of what we did, kind of accepted it went on. It was to their advantage at times. Before the CCS started sticking it to the Rangers mob and their scarfers at Ibrox, Hibs fans got a hell of a time there. Rangers fans would regularly ambush the Hibs scarfers as soon as they got off their supporters buses and Ibrox became virtually a no-go area for Hibs fans. That all changed when we became the focal point for the Rangers attacks and the scarfers, as a result, enjoyed trouble-free travel to and from Ibrox. They would never have admitted it at the time, and they certainly wouldn't confess to it now, but we had more than one scarfer thank us for taking the heat off them.

But Celtic scarfers never saw the benefit of having their casuals bear the brunt of the violence in their stead. Perhaps because there were so many of them, they always enjoyed a numerical advantage. Don't get me wrong, we didn't feel sorry for the Celtic mob because they had never done anything to command our respect in the first place. Hiding among your scarfers then jawing off at the fence once you're inside the ground is the coward's way. But that's what they had done yet again.

We'd employed our usual tactics, hanging out in a bookie's at the corner of Bothwell Street, waiting for them to come along. Someone would be acting as a spotter outside, and give us the shout when the opposition started arriving. But when they wandered out on this day Celtic had got themselves well hidden by the rank and file. Once they were inside the ground, it was following the old familiar pattern. There they were, loud and proud, with a fence protecting them. They were giving it big licks; we were laughing at them and telling them we'd see what happened once we got outside the ground. For some reason they were confident that day. Celtic weren't normally the cockiest of mobs, probably because they feared a hiding from their own kind if they showed-out too much. But on this day they were as bold as brass. And midway through the second half we found out why.

Their mob went quiet but we thought they were just shiting it because the big words would soon have to be backed up by action. Then a canister flew over our heads and landed further up the terracing. I think it was designed to land in among us but they'd cocked up it up and thrown it too far. We knew what it was straight away: it was a CS-gas canister. They'd been bumming for weeks about having bought these things from some pal of theirs in Germany but nobody took them seriously. As soon as it hit the deck the gas started seeping out and before long people were choking and coughing and covering their noses and mouths with scarves. The Celtic mob had made such a mess of it they'd not only missed our mob, but also hadn't even taken the wind into account. There was a breeze swirling around Easter Road that day and it was blowing the gas straight back towards the area where we were and they also were. There were a lot of angry scarfers slap-bang in the firing line and it was getting ugly for the Celtic mob.*

We made a beeline for the pitch because that was the safest place to be and they had done the same thing, because they were being choked by their own gas. We figured they wouldn't dare risk lobbing another CS canister even if they had one with them. And we also reckoned that was the best chance of having a go at them. Their own scarfers were raging with them and set about them. We, meanwhile, were dancing on the pitch, taunting them that their big moment had come to this, getting a doing from their own scarfers.

The Hibs scarfers, who had also been caught in the firing line, weren't best-pleased either. There had been women and kids in that stand as well and they were being treated by first-aid people out on the pitch while the game was stopped. It was getting serious

---

* The *Daily Record* took the view that the CS gas could easily have caused a disaster on the scale of the Heysel stadium outrage in 1985, in which thirty-nine fans were crushed to death. There was a crowd of 23,000 inside Easter Road that day and the terracing was tightly packed with fans. As the paper reported, 'Thousands of panicking fans ran blinded, choking and vomiting, on to the pitch . . . [which was] a sea of bodies.' The *Record* was so concerned by the incident that it ran the story on its front page under the headline 'Work of Morons' and, in a strongly worded editorial, condemned those responsible. AC

for the Celtic mob. There was every chance they were going to get ripped to pieces by the angry mob and the coppers had to pile into the crowd to protect them. This was better than we could ever have imagined. This was Celtic's big day, the day they planned to take the piss out of us and instead they were now under police protection. Once the match had restarted, they remained that way until the final whistle.

We didn't even see the last five minutes because we'd already left the ground and made our way round to the Dunbar End, where we knew Celtic would make their exit. Our timing was out. By the time we got there a huge mob of scarfers was already in place, determined to sort out the gas throwers. All it needed was a few flaming torches, and Dracula's castle in the background, and the picture would have been complete. The scarfers were baying for blood and for once we could stand back and enjoy the fun. The only problem was, with so many scarfers waiting at the exit, there was no way we could lay a hand on Celtic and exact retribution. Vanloads of coppers were pulling up, determined to prevent a riot from taking place. As the Celtic mob appeared, surrounded by coppers, the mob roared and surged forward. This wasn't posturing by the ordinary fans; they were raging and the Celtic mob looked terrified as they were led out.

As ill-conceived stunts go Celtic's ploy took the biscuit, but who knows what they were thinking. If you pull a stroke like that you know you're going to face the wrath of scarfers. It goes with the territory. And if you're not prepared to stand your ground and fight, you just wind up making an arse of yourself, which is precisely what they did. It went from bad to worse for them when the coppers arrested a couple of their boys for the incident. One was charged with bringing the canister into the ground, the other with throwing it. And the defence of the boy who'd carried the gas into

Easter Road was that it was self-defence because he feared being attacked by opposition fans. Standing up in court and claiming you were scared of the opposition mob was as bad as it got for a casual crew. The two jokers got jail time for their stunt and Celtic probably thought that was that but they couldn't have been more wrong. There was no way we were going to ignore the fact they'd come on to our patch and pulled a stroke like that. There would have to be payback.

Our chance came later the same season when they next visited Easter Road. The coppers had put on a show of strength for the occasion, determined they wouldn't be caught on the hop again. The Edinburgh newspapers had been full of the prospects of retribution being taken and it wasn't going to be easy to get at them. Credit to their mob, because at least they came through. I can think of several mobs who would have given it a wide berth under the circumstances.

But they clearly weren't up for it. They had a huge police escort to the ground and we'd anticipated that. This would be a day when violence wasn't the only solution. They'd tried to mess with our minds by lobbing CS gas at us in our own stadium. We'd return the favour. As usual, we were up at the fence to meet them and the verbals were less than pleasant. Feeling a little braver now they were inside the ground, they were taunting us about their last visit. We were reminding them of how the police had saved them from being torn limb from limb. We also warned them that the Edinburgh police weren't their greatest fans after that incident and suggested they might not to be able to rely on their protection if we mounted a charge after the match. They went strangely quiet after that. Mind you, so did we.

It was the usual Celtic visit to Easter Road and they won in a canter. But we had other things on our minds as the match drew to a close. In our own minds, we knew that the threat we'd made of charging the Celtic mob was a non-starter. The coppers were in no mood to have another ugly confrontation between Hibs and Celtic. Too many questions had been asked after the gas incident, with the public demanding to know how a CS canister could be smuggled into a football ground.

We knew we'd have to be clever and we'd scouted the route the cops used to escort their mob to the ground. They'd taken them straight over the hill from Waverley station, along Regent Road. It brought them past the old Scottish Parliament building and was a picturesque route if you had time to enjoy the view. I daresay they didn't because all they would be worrying about was getting into the ground. It seemed a reasonable guess that was also the way they'd be going back and it was perfect for us. They'd have to cross London Road, which would be heaving with traffic at that time on a Saturday night. There would also be a load of fans making their way up Easter Road and it was the ideal ambush point. We'd simply ease our way into the middle of their mob as they headed for Regent Road.

It worked an absolute treat but we weren't planning to get stuck into them because that would be the easiest way to get lifted. As the police escorted them up the road we simply blended in with them in ones and twos. But it was done quickly, very quickly, and their mob was surrounded by us, who were in turn surrounded by the police. Then we really messed with their minds. We patted their arses, stuck our tongues in their ears, made as if to kiss them. The Celtic boys had no idea what was going on. Instead of worrying about being beaten black and blue by the top mob in Scotland, their fear now was that they were going to be raped!

The irony wasn't lost on us. They were being escorted around the side of Calton Hill, one of Edinburgh's best-known gay haunts, and they were worrying that the top mob in Scotland were actually the

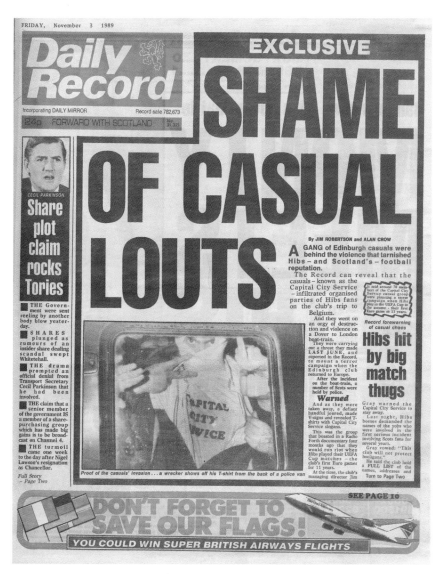

FRIDAY, November 3 1989

Daily Record

Incorporating DAILY MIRROR   Record sale 782,673

24p   FORWARD WITH SCOTLAND

EXCLUSIVE

SHAME OF CASUAL LOUTS

CECIL PARKINSON

Share plot claim rocks Tories

■ THE Government were sent reeling by another body blow yesterday.

■ SHARES plunged as rumours of an insider share dealing scandal swept Whitehall.

■ THE drama prompted an official denial from Transport Secretary Cecil Parkinson that he had been involved.

■ THE claim that a senior member of the government IS a member of a share-purchasing group which has made big gains is to be broadcast on Channel 4.

■ THE turmoil came one week to the day after Nigel Lawson's resignation as Chancellor.

Full Story – Page Two

By JIM ROBERTSON and ALAN CROW

A GANG of Edinburgh casuals were behind the violence that tarnished Hibs – and Scotland's – football reputation.

The Record can reveal that the casuals – known as the Capital City Service – infiltrated organised parties of Hibs fans on the club's trip to Belgium.

And they went on an orgy of destruction and violence on a Dover to London boat-train.

They were carrying out a threat they made LAST JUNE, and reported in the Record, to mount a terror campaign when the Edinburgh club returned to Europe.

After the incident on the boat-train, a number of Scots were held by police.

Warned

And as they were taken away, a defiant handful jeered, made V-signs and revealed T-shirts with Capital City Service slogans.

This was the group that boasted in a Radio Forth documentary four months ago that they would run riot when Hibs played their UEFA Cup matches – the club's first Euro games for 11 years.

At the time, the club's managing director Jim

It said around 70 members of the Capital City Service casual group were planning a terror campaign when Hibs play in the UEFA Cup in the autumn – their first Euro game in 11 years.

Record forewarning of casual chaos

Hibs hit by big match thugs

Gray warned the Capital City Service to stay away.

Last night, Hibs bosses demanded the names of the yobs who were involved in the first serious incident involving Scots fans for several years.

Gray vowed: "This club will not protect hooligans."

He said the club hold a FULL LIST of the names, addresses and Turn to Page Two

Proof of the casuals' invasion . . . a wrecker shows off his T-shirt from the back of a police van

SEE PAGE 10

DON'T FORGET TO SAVE OUR FLAGS!

YOU COULD WIN SUPER BRITISH AIRWAYS FLIGHTS

When Hibs faced FC Liège on 31 October 1989 the CCS caused considerable mayhem in Belgium and on a boat-train from Dover to London. This front-page story is typical of the way in which casuals in general, and the CCS in particular, were portrayed in the media.

(courtesy Mirrorpix)

The early days. The CCS meeting in our 'HQ', the Penny Black pub, just off Princes Street. Sadly, the pub has now closed down.

Mob-handed. The CCS walking down Easter Road before a game. Derek Dykes is in the middle foreground, wearing a light-blue jacket.

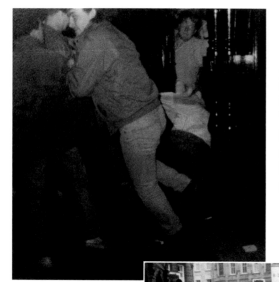

A CCS assault on the Haymarket bar, 'HQ' of the Hearts mob, in 1986. The boy on the ground is a Hearts casual trying desperately to get back into the pub . . . and safety.

The CCS often travelled with its Baby Crew in tow, as this photograph taken near Haymarket station shows.

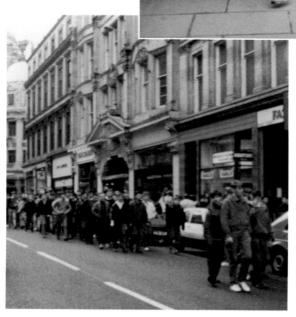

The CCS had many battles with the Rangers mob over the years and is seen here in Glasgow city centre on the way to Ibrox in the mid-to-late eighties.

ARENA OF HORROR

Agony of fans in teargas attack

By HAMISH LEAL and ALEX MURRAY

TERROR came to Easter Road in the 62nd minute of Saturday's Hibs-Celtic match.

A canister of tear gas exploded. Thousands of panicking fans ran, blinded, choking and vomiting on to the pitch.

And yesterday some of the victims among the 23,000 crowd said they were going to die.

Thirteen-year-old Stephen Johnstone, of Musselburgh, was standing on the terracing next to the pitch when he heard a bang "just like a bomb had been dropped."

He said: "I saw everybody just panicking, and so I did the same myself.

"I said to my two friends, 'run, just run' and started running. But I got knocked to the ground, and a man helped me up.

BLOOD

"People were trying to get over the fence and police were getting their truncheons out and hitting young ones until somebody shouted, 'it's tear gas, it's tear gas.'

"Then they" rled to help them out."

The stinging fumes caused agony for this fan ... but help came in the shape of a burly policeman.

Fascist link to big game violence

By IAN BROADLEY

FASCIST-BACKED thugs may be behind the outbreak of smoke bomb-throwing incidents at football matches.

The near-catastrophe at Easter Road was the third outbreak at games in Britain and Europe in the past month.

And the new terror weapon in the arsenal of the ultra-right is the gas canister.

Cypriot 'keeper Andreas Chariou was temporarily blinded by a smokebomb thrown during the recent European Championship game in Holland.

And Yugoslav club Hajduk Split were banned from European competition for two years after a smoke canister was hurled during their Cup-Winners Cup-tie with Olympique Marseilles.

In the aftermath of the Heysel tragedy, a Belgian Government report found that hooliganism is organised on an international scale and paid for by right-wing groups.

And there are specific links between gangs operating in Britain, Belgium and Holland.

Their fascist backers even pay for clothes, travel and tickets to get the thugs across.

Violence

The motive is to destabilise the countries through violence at football, says the report.

A fan arrested recently in Belgium was found to be held in a Danish fascist organisations there.

There was also correspondence linking him with gangs operating in Manchester, Chelsea and Holland.

Easter Road, 28 November 1987. When Celtic casuals threw a CS-gas canister onto crowded terracing it caused panic. Many fans sought refuge on the pitch and observers feared that it could have been a disaster of 'Heysel' proportions. The CCS later took its revenge on the Celtic mob for this outrage.

(courtesy Mirrorpix)

The Aberdeen ASC was Scotland's top mob until it was overtaken by the CCS. In these photos from 1988 the two mobs are fighting on Bothwell Street, close to Easter Road.

Wembley for England–Scotland matches was always a great opportunity to cause mayhem. In 1988 the CCS warmed up with a fight against Chelsea in Leicester Square.

Derek Dykes in the car park at Wembley stadium shortly after the 1988 game with England.

The CCS at New Street station, Birmingham. As well as taking on Aston Villa the CCS made history by becoming the first mob to battle with an ice-hockey team.

Into the lions' den. In 1990 the CCS faced one of their greatest challenges by taking on Millwall on their own patch.

SALUTE OF SHAME!

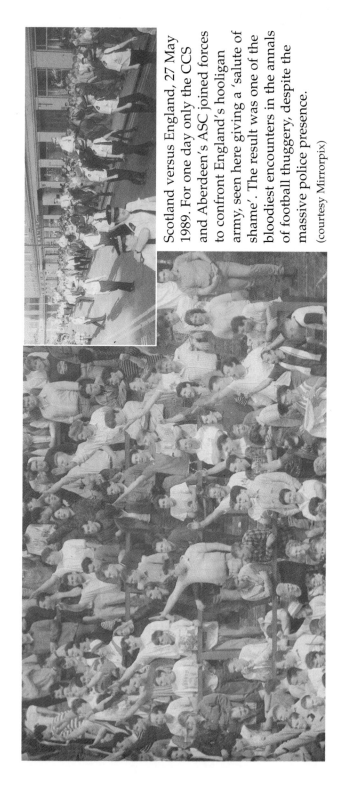

Scotland versus England, 27 May 1989. For one day only the CCS and Aberdeen's ASC joined forces to confront England's hooligan army, seen here giving a 'salute of shame'. The result was one of the bloodiest encounters in the annals of football thuggery, despite the massive police presence.

(courtesy Mirrorpix)

The CCS had been boasting for months about the havoc they would cause if Hibs got back into Europe. Here they are on a stop-off in Brussels before going on to play FC Liège in October 1989.

Enjoying a few beers in Liège before seeing off the home mob.

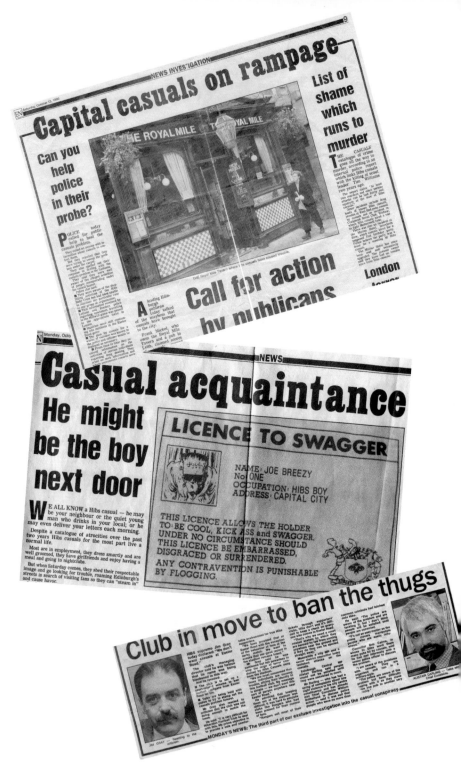

The *Edinburgh Evening News* ran a series of articles on the CCS 'problem' from 13 to 15 October 1990. According to police the 'problem' caused by the mob included murder, an allegation strenuously denied by the CCS.
(courtesy *Edinburgh Evening News*)

On their way to Brussels to face Anderlecht in September 1992 the CCS were enraged to learn that the Rangers mob was attacking Hibs scarfers in Amsterdam. This was a liberty that could not be overlooked and the CCS took vengeance on Rangers. One hapless Rangers boy was so desperate to get away from the fight that he took refuge in the canal!

The Dutch police took a dim view of the CCS battling in Amsterdam and escorted the whole mob to the railway station.

On their way to Anderlecht's stadium in Brussels the CCS decided to stop in the 'Arab' quarter to fight the locals. It turned into a battle for survival. One CCS member had his throat cut and was lucky to survive. In these photos the CCS are seen battling local men.

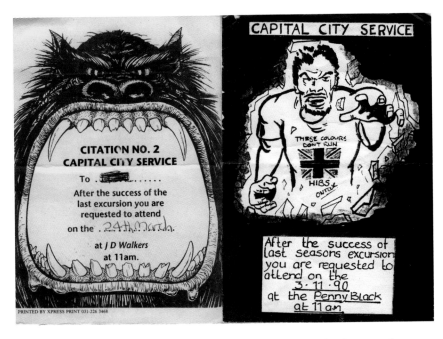

Like most mobs the CCS printed up invitations for its members and new recruits.

PEACE
1990
1990

OFFICIAL CITATION

name: Stevie H

KILL THE

IRN BRU
1 . H

WEGIES

The family requests your presence at the Big Wegie Bash!
10.30am JULES BAR, WATERLOO PLACE
ON THE ___ 10th FEBUARY

WARNING! IF YOU DO NOT ATTEND WITHOUT REASON I.E. DEATH YOU MAY NO LONGER CONSIDER YOURSELF A MEMBER OF THE **C.C.S.**

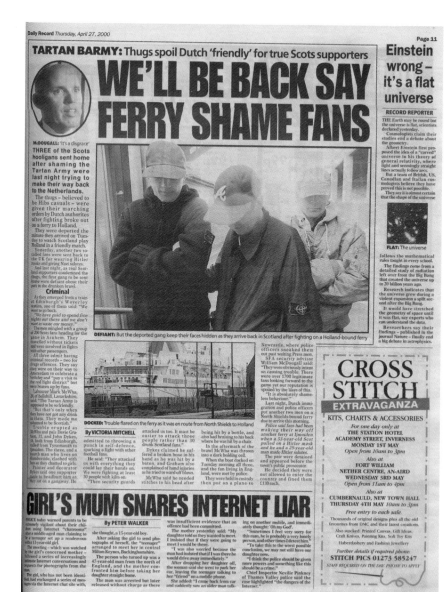

Steaming into the Tartan Army. When Scotland played
Holland in April 2000 the CCS travelled on the same ferry
as the Tartan Army. Given that the CCS consider the Tartan Army
to be creeps a confrontation was inevitable. Derek Dykes is on the
left of this CCS trio.

(courtesy Mirrorpix)

Somehow the CCS, Scotland's most-notorious hooligan gang, managed to blag its way onto Sky Television's *Soccer AM* programme in September 2000. When the *News of the World* found out the paper splashed the story on its front page. This is a video capture from the show and Derek Dykes is on the far right of the back row.

Having renounced violence Derek Dykes is now a family man. He is seen here (*third from the right*) with his arm around his twelve-year-old son Owen as they head to Cork for a pre-season game in 2005.

Derek Dykes outside Easter Road stadium in May 2007, the home of his beloved Hibs.

best-dressed gay group in the country. They suddenly had no certainty about anything because they were being molested and it wasn't pretty. Obviously my stories about the Bar-L hadn't been wasted and I must have told the boys more than they'd let on because they were hamming it up big style. If I hadn't known those guys all my days, I'd have sworn a homosexual gang bang was about to kick off at any moment. I was pissing myself and you could see that, inwardly, so were the boys. Sometimes you see that light dancing in someone's eyes, where they're having a laugh at someone else's expense. That was happening and it was happening in spades. And the problem for Celtic was that they couldn't utter a cheep about it.

The coppers hadn't spotted us joining in with their mob, and we were going quietly about our business. They were oblivious to us and we were being as discreet as possible. And if the Celtic mob cried foul, they'd have less face left than the Invisible Man. It was their choice and their faces were a picture. They were terrified. It must have seemed a long time since they'd felt loud and proud and planned the gas-throwing episode. Now they were trapped in the middle of a bunch of CCS and all they wanted to do was catch a train back to Glasgow. It was never going to be that easy for them. They had a choice. Start it, or ship out of town.

They shipped out.

* * *

The next season they had the chance to get back at us. We went through for a midweek game, purely on a recce. We paid into the Celtic end at Parkhead, just to find out where they hung around. We were betting it would be the Celtic end, because they would have got eaten alive in the Jungle, which was where the seriously mad scarfers went. And we were right. There they were, a little knot of them.

Naturally, we were dressed for the occasion so they clocked us straight away. We could see them locking on to where we were and trying to listen in. We'd decided beforehand we'd pretend to be Scousers but we were crap at the accent. A bunch of boys from Edinburgh can't do Toxteth or Croxteth or any other area of Liverpool. We just sounded like wankers. So the Celtic mob decided they'd have a go and we legged it on to Janefield Street once the gates opened late in the game. Celtic probably felt as though they'd got their pride back that night. I hope they enjoyed that feeling while it lasted.

Next time we went through was when Hibs were playing there. We did our usual. We walked Glasgow, all the way from Queen Street, right up the Gallowgate, until the coppers arrived and moved us to London Road, which was the route visiting fans were meant to take. We were supposed to pay in at the Rangers end. Not a chance. We paid into the Celtic end, and took up our position, the same as we had done for the midweek game. There were thousands more people there but the plan was the same. Let them see us, see if they'd chase. And they did. As soon as the gates were opened with about fifteen minutes to go in the game, they came hard at us.

They probably figured we'd run and they were right. We legged it on to Janefield Street again. Only this time there was a mob of us, and we then turned around and gave them a doing. I know it has since been claimed by one of their guys he got stabbed that day. He didn't. He got a kicking. But the look on their faces was priceless. This wasn't how they planned it. But it was exactly how we'd planned it. Nobody threw CS gas in our stadium and got away with it.

And Celtic learned that the hard way.

10

PUSHING THE BOUNDARY

Fall-outs are never so bitter than when they happen between friends and we'd been good mates with Oldham's Fine Young Casuals for some time. They had come to our games and we had travelled down to their matches. The trouble was that in 1988 Hibs arranged a pre-season friendly against, of all teams, Oldham. And in the casual world the rules are simple. If your team is on the road like that, you take a mob down and you battle with their mob. That's just how it is so we started laying plans for a fight with our pals.

Once we got all the names together there were 150 of us going to make the trip. We'd head down to Manchester by train while the Baby Crew would go by coach, and there was a full busload of them. The way the train schedules worked out we could travel on the day of the game and still have time for a bit of action before the match got underway.

We'd spoken to a couple of the Oldham boys and they said they'd meet us at Piccadilly station in Manchester. They were as good as their word. Of course, it turned out they had an ulterior motive. They asked if we fancied going to Manchester City's pub and turning them over first. You could see their logic. They could get a good mob into Manchester and take out one of their main rivals without getting their hands dirty themselves. But we were always up for it so the Oldham boys took us from the station to the Arndale centre in the middle of Manchester.

It was only a short walk and the boys were buzzing by the time we got there. City's pub was a basement bar called the Brunswick Cellars. For the life of me I can never understand why a mob would use a place like that. You can't see out on to the street, you have no idea who is coming in, you're basically sitting ducks. They tell me it's now a Burton's menswear shop. That's the best use for it because as a pub it was useless for City's mob. The 150 of us trooped into the place and there were about twenty of City sitting there, caught totally unawares. It didn't take us long to batter them because they were badly outnumbered. We wandered back up the stairs and out into the street, feeling a bit let down because it had been a complete waste of time. You don't want massacres, you want a decent battle.

But as were walking along the road some more of City's mob appeared from wherever they'd been. They'd obviously got the word about what had happened in their pub because they were raging. Now this was more like it. They came charging towards us and we weren't about to take a backward step so irresistible force met immovable object. We were steaming into each other, no quarter asked or given, and their fury made them hard boys to handle. The pavement wasn't wide enough to cope with us all and it spilled out into the middle of the street. It was like Paisley Road West all over again. Some folk might be surprised none of us got killed that day, with all the battling that went on. I'm more amazed none of us got knocked down because every two minutes we were on one busy road or another, with traffic flying past at a rate of knots.

But for all City were very game, there were just too many of us and we wound up giving their mob a second doing in a very short space of time. They turned and ran and we chased them all over the centre of Manchester. As the whole thing spread through the city centre, with CCS boys running this way and that after City, shoppers were diving for cover. That never goes on for long in a city centre because someone always calls the coppers. As soon as we heard the sirens of the police cars coming from all sides our mob regrouped before the coppers arrived. We were all rounded up and taken back to Piccadilly station. Then they put us on the train to Oldham.

We were cutting it fine to make the start of the match because the City battle had taken longer than we'd expected. But that was a minor irritation compared to the problems faced by the Baby Crew. Their coach had gone straight to Oldham while we were busy battling in Manchester. They got dropped off in the middle of town and they wandered around for a bit before heading towards the ground. As they were making their way along the street they passed a pub, which, unknown to them, was full of the Oldham mob. They were spotted and the Oldham crew came charging out, ready to stick it to their old pals. Now given that the Baby Crew were expecting 150 of us to be in Oldham by the time they got there, it must have come as a hell of a shock when they found out they were on their own against Oldham's entire mob. But fair play to them, even some of the Oldham boys would admit in later years that they fought like tigers. They stood, they didn't run, but Oldham got the better of them and one or two got a right beating. That was it as far as Oldham were concerned. Their chests were puffed out after that. They thought they'd battered our main mob and they were full of themselves. They didn't realise they'd only done our Baby Crew. Christ, don't people in these mobs talk to each other? Two of their guys had met us off the train but presumably they'd been working to their own agenda in getting us to do City.

Just after the Baby Crew fight with Oldham the coppers turned up and they escorted our young team to Oldham's ground, Boundary Park. Oldham were following them and hurling abuse about the way they'd been beaten. It was all 'We thought you were meant to be hard', that sort of stuff. In the meantime, we'd got off the train at Oldham station and we were just going to make it on time. It must have been about 2:50 or even 2:55 by the time our 150-strong mob appeared outside Boundary Park. It was one of those old grounds, just like Stark's Park, where you could see out into the street and their mob were right up at the top of the terracing.

We couldn't work out why they looked so worried when they saw us arriving but they looked gobsmacked. Reality was dawning on them that they hadn't battered our mob, but our Baby Crew, and they looked shit-scared. Once we got inside the ground and found the Baby Crew we learned what had happened and we were seething. There was a fence separating the fans and we were up against it in an instant with them on the other side. We told them, 'So you think you have fucking done us, do you? You only did our Baby Crew, and now we'll see what happens after the game.'

The coppers inside the ground could sense there was trouble in the air and so could the Hibs scarfers, because about two thousand of them had come down as well. They were giving us a wide berth but the coppers had their own plan to defuse the tension. The way the Boundary Park terracing was set up was like big metal pens. There were lines of fences running from the back of the terracing to the front and at the back of the terracing there were gates that could be locked. A whole mob of police appeared just before kick-off, and they were obviously going to try and lock the gate on the section of the ground we were in. We clocked them and we charged because we were having none of that. We knew that if that gate got locked at any point during the ninety minutes our day was over. The police would just keep us penned in there, steaming mad, for about twenty minutes after the final whistle and make sure Oldham had dispersed before they'd even let us out of the ground. That was not going to happen.

As determined as we were to prevent that happening, the police were equally determined to get that damned gate locked. We fought a running battle with them throughout the ninety minutes because we were gagging for a shot at Oldham after what they'd done to the Baby Crew. And, unlike the players on the pitch, we didn't get a break at half-time for a cup of tea. It was full on with the coppers throughout the match and it was brutal stuff. They were going at us with truncheons and we were hammering at them with fists and boots. In the end, we won our battle. That gate remained unlocked. The coppers switched to Plan B. They closed off other connecting gates so that all the fans would leave the ground by one set of exits while we would be channelled down towards two huge, wooden exit gates, which would remain locked. What was it with Oldham and bloody gates?

With about ten minutes of the match remaining Oldham must have got the word from the coppers to get out because Plan B was in operation. We knew something was up because the coppers we'd been battling with for the entire match had suddenly backed off, and they were smiling. As we looked down at the street we could see Oldham massing outside the ground. We poured out of the still-open metal gate into a big open area behind the turnstiles. We were looking for a way out and then we spotted the big wooden gates, slammed shut. They must have been twelve-to-fourteen-foot-high and they were solid. The cops still had us penned in. They'd just done it in a different area of the ground and once we'd all bolted through the gate at the top of the terracing, they finally got that locked so we couldn't even go back that way and cause mayhem elsewhere.

No wonder those coppers had been smiling as they beat a tactical retreat. We'd been done-up good and proper. But there had to be a way of getting these bastards back. The boys were getting restless, we all were, because no one likes having the piss taken out of them and that was what was happening here. Oldham weren't even prepared to fight us on their own patch. That lacked class. Instead, their mob were outside the ground, chanting and taunting because they thought they were home free.

I climbed up onto one of the turnstile roofs and another of our mob did the same. At least from there you could get a view of what was going on outside. Oldham must have felt very safe. About forty yards from the wooden gates there was a line of coppers and behind them stood the Oldham mob, about two hundred of them making plenty of noise. There was nothing else for it. We had to break our way through those gates. Taking the aerial route over the turnstiles wasn't an option because we could only go over in ones and twos and once we'd landed on the street Oldham would have made mincemeat of us.

Breaking the gates it was and our guys launched themselves at them. As soon as the first bang on the gates was heard outside the Oldham boys burst out laughing. Then a copper came right up under the turnstiles to tell me we were wasting our time. Manchester City's mob had been caught the same way before and they'd tried to force open those gates. They had failed so the coppers were confident we wouldn't succeed. That's when I thought, 'Oldham must have pulled this stroke before'.

But the guys weren't about to give in and every time they charged at those gates you could hear this loud creak, almost as if the gates themselves were in pain. Oldham were going mental outside, singing, dancing, pointing. Gloating. We climbed off the turnstile roofs and joined in the assault on the gates. Jesus, these bloody things were solid. Your body took the full shock of the collision every time you hit them. I could have sworn my fillings were working loose. We were knackered, absolutely knackered, but we gave it one last go. The gates burst open and we were through screaming 'CCS!' You've never heard singing stop so quickly.

Most of the Oldham mob scattered, because they couldn't believe we were out of the ground. The coppers were just as surprised and they were first in the firing line because they had been standing in front of the Oldham crew. They just stood there, transfixed. So did a few of the Oldham boys, who looked as though they were in shock. As we came pouring through those gates we were like the hounds of hell. It was a bloodbath, an absolute bloodbath, as the pent-up frustration of being locked in the ground was released. There were battered bodies all over the place because we really laid into them. They didn't stand a chance.

Their top boy was still standing in the middle of the street, and, to give him his due, he didn't run. Compared to the rest of his mob he did quite well but we just flew right over the top of him and in the end he got a bad beating. We came out of it pretty well unscathed. A few of the boys got arrested but that was it. That was also it for the friendship with Oldham. They didn't invite us back after that.

I wonder why.

* * *

At least by the time we finally fell out with Oldham we'd been friendly for a few years. Believe me, we fell out with a good few English mobs in a lot less time than that because so many of them were vastly overrated. In real terms, they were playing at it.

A few Newcastle boys used to come up to Hibs back in 1984 or 1985 when the whole casual thing was really kicking off in Scotland. We'd go down there as well and the two mobs got on pretty well together. They invited us down to their patch one time when they were playing Manchester United. Everybody wanted extra bodies when they were playing Manchester United because they had a massive mob. With the game being played at St James' Park, Newcastle didn't want to be shown up on their home turf so that's why we got the invitation.

Around forty or fifty of us got the train down to Newcastle and we met up with their mob. This was back in the days when you paid in at the gate, you didn't need tickets to get in and it was easier for us to go into the 'wrong' end. The main body of the Newcastle support was at the famous Gallowgate end while Manchester United fans were given the terracing at the opposite end of the ground, behind the goal. The object of the exercise was to give Man U a hiding so it seemed obvious to us to pay into the United end. And that's exactly what we did.

It was about ten minutes into the game and we couldn't see any sign of the Newcastle mob so we made our way to the fence separating the two sets of fans because that's where the mobs always hung about. Sure enough, the Manchester United mob were on our side of it but Newcastle's mob were on the other side.

The Newcastle mob were shouting about what was going to happen after the game, telling them what a doing they were going to get. That made no sense to us. Just looking at the size of Man United's crew, surprise was the only option you had. Telling them you were coming for them after the game seemed like a short cut to a beating. So we positioned ourselves alongside them and, as soon as 'CCS' was chanted, we steamed in.

By the time the coppers realised the fighting had started there was chaos in the United end. It had been jam-packed and people were trying to get out of the way of the battle. Because the cops had to squeeze past a mass of bodies to get to the heart of the battle we got a good five minutes of scrapping in before it was halted. We did well; we took a few of them down and got out of it ourselves with just the usual cuts and scrapes. A couple of the boys were arrested and the rest of us got chucked out of the ground.

When we met up with the Newcastle mob later we were feeling pretty pleased with ourselves. They, on the other hand, looked as though they had been sucking lemons. It turned out some of their older boys weren't at all happy with us. They thought we had been disrespectful to them as the host mob because we had taken the lead. I'd never heard so much rubbish in all my life. Disrespectful? They wanted a battle with them, and we'd gone and had a battle with them while they stood hurling insults from the other side of the fence. If we could do it, why couldn't they? They weren't having it. If we were on their patch, we had to do things their way, they said. We were tempted to have a go at them, there and then, and tempers were fraying. But we went back up the road with a fragile peace still in place, although we were calling them for everything on the train.

And, what do you know, within a few weeks we were back in Newcastle. We didn't even bother waiting on an invitation, simply because they were playing West Ham. West Ham's crew, the Inter City Firm, were one of the top mobs in Britain. The chance to scrap with the ICF was too good to pass up. We put together a handy mob, about a hundred, and the boys went down by train, bus or van.

We all met up before heading to Newcastle's pub to offer them our services but they were ungrateful bastards, they really were. The reception we got was as frosty as a polar bear's backside. This time they were unhappy we'd brought so many boys with us. Jesus, there was no pleasing some folk. After what we'd seen of them against Manchester United we thought they'd be grateful for the help. Not a bit of it. They were bitching and moaning that we were trying to run their show. What show? There wouldn't have been one the last time without us. I could see that a few of the boys who hadn't made the trip down to Newcastle the last time were wondering what was going on and wondering why they had even bothered making the trip. But Newcastle or no Newcastle, we were going to have a go.

Sadly, the whole day turned out to be a damp squib. I thought I knew all about police escorts until I saw the sort of numbers who were in place for West Ham. It was wall-to-wall police. We couldn't get near them and their end was strictly West Ham only. There wasn't a prayer of getting in there. We hung around the train station after the match in the hope of getting a run at them but there was nothing doing. The coppers had a ring of steel round them. There were a few verbals exchanged but that was about it. What a waste of a Saturday. Still, at least we knew where we stood with Newcastle now and they could forget about any link-up with us in the future.

We did actually bump into the Newcastle mob again.

They'd travelled north for the Scotland versus England international in 1989, coming up the east-coast main line. They broke their journey home in Edinburgh, presumably thinking they'd see some familiar faces in Princes Street. They did, but things had moved on in the past few years. We were the top mob in Scotland by then and we'd been battling with the English at Hampden that day. And now, here they were, walking down Princes Street. Big, big mistake.

We went for them and they started running but they knew they were done for. When we caught up with them a lot of what they got went back four years to when they'd accused us of disrespecting them. So they didn't want us running their show down in Newcastle? Well, now they were finding out how we ran our show in Edinburgh. And I don't think they liked it much.

All ties were finally severed.

* * *

Newcastle weren't the only north-east mob we had no time for.

Before the battle of Boundary Park, when we ended our association with Oldham, their mob had asked us to meet up with them before their game at Sunderland. Oldham told us they were bringing a huge mob because it was going to be a tear-up.

We arranged to meet them at the train station in Newcastle and we took about forty boys with us. When we reached Newcastle we found the Oldham boys but there were only twenty-five of them. We were already wondering if this was going to be another wasted journey to Newcastle.

The Oldham boys explained there should have been another hundred of them, who were travelling separately, but that the coppers had got wind of it and stopped them boarding the train. The coppers had got wind of more than that. They pounced on us in the station and rounded up the CCS boys. Oldham's planning must have been seriously dodgy to have the coppers on to them so quickly. The police weren't wasting any time. There was an Edinburgh train due into the station at any minute and they were planning to put us on it and send us homeward to think again. They shoved us into the carriage and walked away. And we all climbed out of the window in the door on the other side of the carriage, dropped on to the train tracks and legged it out of the station. We nipped back in time to catch the train to Sunderland and the Oldham boys were on it.

There was supposed to a battle arranged but it was all quiet before the game. But as we came out of Roker Park after the match, Sunderland were waiting. They had a decent mob but, to be honest with you, they couldn't fight sleep. Oldham were happy for us to take the lead with them following on behind and the joint mob charged at Sunderland. There was a long road that led from Roker Park all the way back to the station and it became the battleground. Sunderland were a poor excuse for a crew; I don't know why

Oldham needed us because they'd fight, then run, then fight, then run and we were giving them a hiding.

The coppers maybe thought they'd headed off the trouble by sticking us on the train at Newcastle but, for whatever reason, they were slow on the scene that day, which was bad news for Sunderland. We were practically at the station before the coppers showed up. We pulled off straight away because this was Oldham's fight and the coppers split them and Sunderland. Oldham were kept outside the station while Sunderland were sent down on to the platform. We just wandered into the station unnoticed because the cops were so focused on the Oldham boys. Once we got on to the platform it all kicked off again and only the arrival of the train back to Newcastle saved Sunderland from another hiding. Even with half a mob we were giving them a doing.

Most of the Sunderland boys had to get trains back to Newcastle before catching another train on to wherever in the north-east they lived. When Sunderland boarded the train we got on the same carriage while the police brought the Oldham boys down and stuck them in the guard's van. We were going to kick it off again but the Sunderland mob had taken enough by then and they had nothing left. I think they were grateful that we stopped when we did but it would have been taking liberties to keep going. We'd battered them. Their top boy said to us, 'You've got a good mob.'

Then he made us an offer we most definitely could refuse. 'Like I said,' he repeated, 'you've got a good mob. How do you fancy coming back down here on Wednesday? We're playing Leeds.' Fighting Leeds with the whole of the CCS in tow. Fine. Fighting Leeds as guests of a poor Sunderland crew? Not fine.

We told him straight that if Sunderland couldn't stand against forty Hibs and twenty-five Oldham, they didn't have a cat in hell's chance against Leeds. We thanked him for the offer, because it was nice to be asked, but there was no way we were taking him up on it. The Magnificent Seven would have turned that one down. We'd been on enough suicide missions of our own without having useless crews dream up more for us. We never heard on the grapevine whether the Sunderland–Leeds fight ever materialised. If it did, I know who my money would have been on.

And it certainly wouldn't have been the crew from Roker Park.

11

THE IRRITATING MR WELSH

By the late 1980s we were Scotland's top mob; I don't think anyone seriously questioned that. We'd gone the whole hog by then. T-shirts had been made up with the phrase 'These Colours Don't Run, Hibs Casuals on Tour'. A second T-shirt bearing the message 'Joe Breezy, Licence to Swagger' was also on the go. It bore the words, 'This licence allows the holder to be cool, kick ass and swagger. Under no circumstances should this licence be embarrassed, disgraced or surrendered. Any contravention is punishable by flogging.' Invitation cards had also been printed, stating the times and dates of meetings.

But these were just things to keep the boys amused. When it came to the serious business we'd taken on Rangers and won, half of Aberdeen's top boys were in jail, and there was nobody else out there really. Except the Motherwell Saturday Service, of course, who still thought they could have a say in the matter. They came to our patch on 31 December 1988 to see out the old year with a league game against Hibs. We paid into the old Dunbar End at Easter Road for that game and their mob didn't even spot us. And we stood very quietly, minding our own business, not singing, doing absolutely nothing. You really would have thought they'd have clocked us but not a bit of it. I guarantee you if their mob had been anywhere near us we'd have spied them in an instant but they were oblivious to our presence. Until Hibs scored the only goal of the game, that is. We went mental because the Hibees had scored. They went mental because they finally realised we were in their end. That was the cue for another terracing battle and they were game, I'll give you that. But so were we and force of numbers wore them down. Strike one for Hibs. Happy New Year.

Within twenty-eight days Hibs had seen off Brechin in the Scottish Cup and when the draw was made later that night, guess what? Hibs were drawn at home to Motherwell. We figured they wouldn't fancy it, given the fact they'd copped a doing on Hogmanay. Instead, it turned out they did, at least that was what we were hearing. The word on the grapevine was that the Motherwell SS were telling the world and his brother, and even several of his cousins, how they were going to bring a serious mob through to Easter Road for the cup-tie and even the score. We knew this because one of our mob was from Motherwell and he had heard them jawing off about how they were going to do Hibs.

The Motherwell SS were always good at talking themselves up. Their biggest problem was that they didn't know how to keep their traps shut when they couldn't be sure who was listening. We only discussed CCS business in the company of CCS members, especially plans for future battles. The last thing you need is some big-eared copper, or one of the opposition, getting the drop on you.

It's probably just as well we adhered to that system or Irvine Welsh would have had even more to write about. Ask any CCS fella what irritates him more than anything and it's seeing Irvine Welsh described as a former Hibs casual. It's maybe because he has contributed to books like *Terrace Legends* (edited by Cass Pennant, a real hard man), inadvertently giving some people who don't know any better the impression that he was one of us. I have even been described in the press as a friend of Irvine Welsh, which is strange as I have never spoken to the man. Let's get this straight. If Irvine Welsh has ever claimed to be a Hibs casual, at any point in his life, he's an impostor. None of us begrudge him the cash he's made from *Trainspotting* and his other books, good luck to him. But he wasn't a casual. He might have hung around the pubs in which casuals congregated but he wasn't out there when the fists and boots were flying. So let's lay that one to rest.

But we had our answer to Irvine Welsh, our Motherwell CCS man, and he'd come up with the goods. Not only had the Motherwell SS been mouthing off about what they were going to do, but also every last detail was out there in the public domain. We were informed that their bus was leaving from a street just round the corner from Motherwell's ground, Fir Park. We even knew the time they were planning to leave, eleven o'clock. Perfect. Absolutely perfect.

The day before the cup-tie we hired ten Transit vans, all from different van-rental shops around Edinburgh. That way it caused less suspicion and the rental company were less likely to flag it up to the coppers that a bunch of casuals had hired a fleet of vans. The coppers knew fine that if we were hiring vans it could only mean one thing – that we were off for a ruck somewhere. So we spread our business around and packed a mob of fifty into the hired vans on the morning of the cup-tie for the journey through to Motherwell. They were going to even up the score were they? We'd see about that.

Our boy had given us directions to exactly where they'd be so we knew exactly where we were going. The biggest problem was finding a space big enough to take ten Tranny vans when we parked them up. As luck would have it there was a big car dealership near the ground and that was ideal. We parked there because we figured a fleet of vans wouldn't look so suspicious parked at a car lot. Our Motherwell boy took a stroll round the corner to see if their mob was around and the timing was perfect.

There they were, large as life, getting ready to board their buses for the journey to Edinburgh. He gave us the signal and we were off. We came flying round the corner at them and they were frozen in shock. We'd caught them absolutely stone cold and there was sheer panic etched all over their faces because the last thing they expected to see was us on their patch on the morning of a game. It wasn't a fierce battle and it didn't last long. One of their boys got stabbed with a screwdriver and we kicked the crap out of the rest of them. We destroyed them and the message was simple. Don't talk the talk if you can't walk the walk.

We knew what the script would have been at Easter Road anyway. They'd have hidden behind a police escort and done all their jawing when they were safe behind their fence. That was their way. But there's also a police station close to Motherwell's ground so we couldn't hang about because they were screaming for ambulances and police and any of the emergency services that sprang to mind. We scarpered sharpish back to the Transit vans, the plan being to get back through to Edinburgh, have a pint and wait for Motherwell to turn up for round two.

But for reasons best known to himself, the driver of the van I was in started panicking. Rather than take the direct route back to Edinburgh, which is only about half an hour's drive, he was convinced the coppers would have set up roadblocks and God knows what else. I think he'd been watching too many war movies. He was off his head and there was no convincing him. We were screaming at him that the Motherwell mob wouldn't even be able to tell the cops what we were driving because they had neither seen

THESE COLOURS DON'T RUN

us arrive nor leave, but this guy was having none of it. He was adamant we had to take a detour to get back without getting nicked.

We wound up going through Biggar of all places. It's a nice enough town but it's in the middle of bloody nowhere. We were peering out of those daft wee windows you get in the rear doors of a Transit van thinking, 'Where the fuck is he going?' but his mind had gone. He was convinced there would be flashing blue lights in the mirrors any second. It took us two hours to get back to Edinburgh; two hours! We made a mental note that the driver would be a passenger on our next expedition.

By the time we got back we barely had time for a celebratory pint before it was time to regroup. We still had to man the battle stations for round two. Because we knew Motherwell had their bus booked we waited at the top of Easter Road for them because that's the way they would come after the cops had parked them up. And we waited. And we waited. They didn't turn up. So much for levelling the score. To make matters even better, Hibs won the game.

Now you might think that, having had such a successful day, we'd have been content to kick back and bask in the glory of both our and our team's success that night. Sensible people would have done that but who said we were sensible? Around that time, the rave scene was pretty big and some of us were right into it. Our Motherwell boy was one, I was another and there was a place in Motherwell called the Garrion hotel. It had a club in it, which was holding a rave that night. We really fancied going but our Motherwell boy wasn't sure. He said the SS boys would be raging about being embarrassed in their own town and it probably wasn't a good idea. But I told him if he was game for it, so was I and he was happy enough to drive the Transit van, which we hadn't yet returned to the rental place because our driver had gone loopy.

So that was it. There was me, him and a third fella who was just as daft as us. And we were on our way to a nightclub in Motherwell. I admit it wasn't the smartest idea we'd ever had and it didn't take us too long to realise it. We took the precaution of parking the van at the back door of the hotel, just in case things got a bit hairy and we had to make a sharp exit. As we made our way up the street to the front door, we were wishing we'd parked it closer. The SS were out in force and they were all standing outside the entrance to the club. They were looking a bit battered and bruised and they were probably looking to batter someone, any-one, to get something out of a miserable day. You can imagine their reaction when they saw the three of us swaggering up. To say they weren't happy to clap eyes on us again is an understatement.

We'd only just got to the door when the fighting started and they were really going for it. Before any serious damage could be done the bouncers hauled us inside the club and we figured that was that. The fact that they'd been hanging about outside the club, we thought, meant they'd been knocked back at the door and couldn't get inside to have another go. Wrong! We were sitting there having a drink when they came in mob-handed and armed with pool cues. Punters were sent flying in all directions as the SS came charging across the dance floor swinging these pool cues at us. We were already on the move. I was running across a line of chairs and our Motherwell boy was running parallel to me across a row of tables. The two of us just launched ourselves over the bar and landed in a heap behind it.

The third boy had also run but they were closer to him. He tried to dive over the bar as well but as he was in mid-air they stabbed him in the arse. The bouncers waded in before they could plunge him again because he was just hanging there, on top of the bar, saying, 'Christ, they've stabbed me in the arse, they've stabbed me in the arse.' It was just as well the bouncers got there in time because he was stuck there on top of the bar, moaning about his stabbed arse. Poor bugger, we were lying there pissing ourselves with laughter. Obviously he didn't find it funny, but we thought it was hilarious.

The bouncers kicked Motherwell through the front door and smuggled us out the back. Thanks to our initial foresight we made it back to the van no bother, even with our mate hobbling along slowly clutching his wounded arse. Poor guy, he couldn't sit down at all on the journey back to Edinburgh. He was fine once we got him to hospital and got him patched up and even he saw the funny side in the end. It had been a close shave but we were home free.

Strike another one for the CCS.

12

BATTLE OF BRITAIN

'Stopping the game would be sad but these levels of violence can't be seen to continue.'

John Maxton MP, whose Cathcart constituency was home
to Hampden Park

'Wherever it's played this game seems to attract trouble and that's more than it's worth.'

Brian Wilson MP, Labour's spokesman for Scottish sport

Scotland versus England, even England versus Scotland. It didn't matter which of the two countries was hosting the fixture, it meant trouble with a capital T. There had been calls for years for the fixture to be scrapped because England's fans had been beating the crap out of the Tartan Army whenever they got the chance. But by the time England were due to travel north to play at Hampden Park on 27 May 1989 in the Sir Stanley Rous Cup, Scotland were no longer sitting ducks. The problem was that the England mob didn't realise it.

In the weeks leading up the fixture, all the chatter from down south was about how they were coming up to Glasgow to give us a right doing. They still didn't respect Scottish mobs, despite the fact we'd been down there and proved ourselves. The heavy hitters from London were on their way, with Chelsea and West Ham leading the charge. There were mobs from the Midlands and from the north-west making the trip. All these guys were planning to meet up in Glasgow. There was even talk the Rangers mob would be hooking up with them. The north-east mobs were coming via Edinburgh. Sunderland, Middlesbrough and Leeds were coming that way, bolstered by sundry waifs and strays from other mobs.

The police were promising there would be an unparalleled presence on the streets of Glasgow to keep the peace. They could have cancelled police leave right across Britain that day and put them all in Glasgow. It wouldn't have made a blind bit of difference. The battle that eventually took place would have happened regardless of how many coppers there were on the streets. It had been brewing for months.

If you want evidence of how seriously Scottish mobs were taking it, our mob agreed to link up with Aberdeen, for one day only. The two of us needed each other because the numbers arriving from down south would have been too much for one mob to handle on their own. And if Rangers were going to turn traitor and fight alongside the English, we'd be even more badly outnumbered. But the rules for any link-up with the Aberdeen crew were simple. As Scotland's top mob we'd call the shots and if they didn't like that, it was no deal. They went along with that so we were all set for the Battle of Britain.

The plan was simple enough. We knew the English mobs would come to Glasgow on the overnight train and arrive early in the morning, so we'd leave them stewing on their arrival. The Aberdeen mob would catch the first train down on the day of the game and keep out of the way near Queen Street. We would try to intercept the north-east mobs in Edinburgh first, before making our way through to Glasgow to hook up with Aberdeen. If we could do some damage before we even set off for Glasgow, it would give us a leg up.

On the Saturday morning we were out early, prowling around Princes Street and looking for any sign of the incoming mob. We didn't have to wait long. We heard them before we saw them as the chants of 'England, England' wafted up from Waverley station. And then we saw them, swaggering up the ramp from the station, leering at passers-by and wandering around our city as if they owned the place. Well, that was never going to happen.

We wanted every last one of them out of the station before we made our move because any of them who managed to escape would be in Glasgow ahead of us and spreading the word that Scottish mobs were for real. As soon as the whole lot of them were making their way across Princes Street, two hundred of us came roaring at them. Shoppers scattered as we attacked the middle of the line, the classic CCS tactic. One lot of England legged it along Princes Street, the other lot ran off towards St Andrew's Square. We also split as the fighting started in earnest. A group of us headed off in pursuit of the breakaway fans and the geographical advantages were all ours. This was our city. We knew every street, every alley. They had no idea where they were going and we knew they'd try and double back to join up with the rest of their mob. That was their biggest mistake because as soon as they tried to cut along a side street we had them cornered just off St Andrew's Square. We piled in, no holding back. They were backed up against a wall with nowhere to run and they were forced to fight. The guy I was facing caught me unawares but instead of aiming for my face he was hammering away at my arm. I had no idea what he was up to and I wasn't hanging around to find out. If he didn't want to take advantage of his free shot I'd take it for him and I smacked him square in the face. He crumpled and it was on to the next guy.

It was a battle that didn't last long but it was brutal while it did. The English boys were fighting through fear. The confidence they'd felt as they swaggered out of the station evaporated the moment they were ambushed by a huge mob. You could see it in their eyes. They were a long way from home and they were getting a hiding. By the time the coppers arrived on the scene, the battle was all but done. We were off our marks before they arrived, and they were left with nothing but a bunch of bloodied England fans to deal with.

It was only as we were making our way to Princes Street to hook up with the rest of our mob that one of my mates asked me what had happened to my jacket. I was wearing a heavy black leather jacket and as I looked down at the left sleeve I could see that it had practically been shredded. There were five or six puncture marks in it and it was only the fact that the leather was so thick that saved me. It had absorbed the force of the knife. Now I knew why that guy had been hammering at my arm. He'd been trying to stab me. Jesus, if he'd connected with those blows my arm would have been mangled. I'd had another lucky escape.

The Princes Street fight was going great guns by the time we got there. We had to shove our way through frightened shoppers to get at the action and most stores had locked their doors, with hundreds of people trapped inside, looking on in disbelief at the madness taking place outside. There was nowhere for the traffic to go, it was at a standstill as well and that meant it would take the coppers time to get there on foot.

It was perfect for us. We had a good few minutes left to get steamed in and sort out the England mob's eastern flank before heading to Glasgow. That's exactly what we did. We took them apart with the minimum of fuss and while the coppers were busy fighting their way through the traffic to get to us, we'd mingled with the shoppers and slipped off quietly to Waverley station. We had an appointment with our sworn enemies in Glasgow. And we were also due to fight England.

By the time we disembarked from the train in Glasgow, Queen Street station was swarming with coppers. The main mob of English had already pitched up at Central station and the police had presumably been warned by their counterparts in the south that there was a crew on the way up the east-coast main line as well. They'd be sorely disappointed if they were waiting on the north-east boys. A load of them were in hospital, a good number more would have been nicked and the rest were badly beaten up.

We headed to our meeting place with Aberdeen, in George Square, just round the corner from the station. There was no way of telling how this was going to go because we didn't even like each other. There was every chance it could kick off the moment we walked out of the station and we were ready for Aberdeen taking a cheap shot at us. It didn't happen. The atmosphere wasn't cordial; there was neither back-slapping nor even polite handshakes. We were two mobs who despised each other but for this one day we would put that to one side and set about teaching the English a lesson that was long overdue.

Once again, the pecking order was reiterated. Hibs called the shots. When we said go, we'd go. The one concession was that we'd chant CCS when it was time to attack. Aberdeen could still do the 'Come on Aberdeen' bit for their guys. It was an exercise in saving face for them but we were both mindful of the fact that each mob was relying on the other to get through this battle. We knew there would be precious little chance of getting near the English as they left the centre of Glasgow because they would be surrounded by coppers. This was going to be as much about taking the coppers by surprise as about battling the English. We'd be there or thereabouts whenever the English were on the move. The first time the coppers dropped their guard, we'd be in.

Our cause wasn't helped by the fact there were a load of Scotland fans desperate to have a go as well. The newspapers had been having a field day in the build-up to the match, printing stories about a thousand English coming north with the National Front and Combat 18 and all the usual suspects supposedly involved. To be fair, as the English were being shepherded out of the city centre and up Eglinton Toll towards the south side of Glasgow, there were plenty of fascist salutes and shouts of 'Sieg Heil'. Maybe these mobs were part of it after all. We weren't bothered one way or the other. Our fight wasn't political. It was personal.

As the line of England fans snaked its way around a corner and on to Victoria Road, we sensed we might have a chance of attacking but were frustrated again. There was also a line of coppers keeping us on the opposite side of the road from the English and one false move here would mean being nicked for certain. The boys were itching to get into it and so were Aberdeen. As the police took the English on to Victoria Road our chance came. The cops temporarily corralled them at a petrol station while they regrouped before moving them on towards the ground. We charged. We first broke our own police line and ran straight at the line of cops protecting the English. The English were screaming at us to come ahead and we needed no second invitation.

The cops were already on the radio calling in reinforcements as the first wave of Scots washed over them. We pounded into the English, no mercy, and they pounded back. There was a flash of metal close by me and then a grunt as it met its target but you had no time to think. All you were doing was hitting them before they hit you and the English were well up for it. Unlike the boys we'd fought in Edinburgh that morning, these jokers were serious. They didn't budge an inch, and they dished out as much as they took.

The fight was spilling along Victoria Road because the police had to beat a retreat once they were overpowered. But as the battle continued there were English disappearing here, there and everywhere. They'd seized the opportunity to get off their mark and slip the police escort, no doubt intent on causing mayhem on their way to the ground. We also extricated ourselves, as did Aberdeen, because the coppers would be looking for revenge when they finally got their reinforcements. Truncheons cracking heads would be the order of the day and I wasn't hanging around for that. We'd achieved what we set out to do. We'd got the English away from the coppers. Now it was a case of hunting them down.

Once again, it didn't take us long. As we wandered up Victoria Road we spotted a pub jammed to the gunnels with people. At first we figured they were Scotland fans tanking up before the clash with the Auld Enemy. But when we eased the door open a fraction to have a listen the accents were unmistakeably English. Cheeky bastards! They'd done a runner to the nearest boozer and holed up there. Within seconds their bolt hole was minus windows as bricks rained down on the building.

Time for round two. They came flying out the doors, some of them with blood streaming down their faces where they had been cut by flying glass. And, this time, we could quite clearly see that they were well tooled up. Knives, knuckledusters, hammers, iron bars; you name it, they had it. These boys weren't here on a sightseeing trip. Some of our mob still had bricks left over from trashing the pub and within seconds the sky was black with objects being hurled at the English from all angles. It set them back on their heels long enough for us to fire in again, leading with the boot instead of the fist to cut down on the chance of getting stabbed. I'd had one lucky escape on the day. I wasn't gambling on a second.

We went at it again but a couple of our boys weren't so lucky and they did get stabbed, although not seriously. But it was enough to take them out of the action and now the English were really up for it. They were charging up the road taking on all-comers. Tartan Army punters, shoppers, shopkeepers, they were all getting it from the English. No-one resident in Scotland, or who even knew someone resident in Scotland, was safe from this lot. They were looking to cause the maximum damage, and they weren't shy about doing it. They had us pursuing them with the coppers also trying to catch up but being hampered by having to deal with the trail of destruction they were encountering.

We caught up with the English again further up Victoria Road and round three got under way. It was every bit as brutal as rounds one and two and was becoming a war of attrition. Unknown to us the cops had been forced to close Victoria Road because there was no way it was safe for traffic. There were people battling in the middle of the street, there were missiles being hurled, anything that wasn't nailed down was flying through the air. Two main streets closed in Scotland's two major cities in one day. No wonder MPs would later ask questions in the House of Commons.

The look on the English faces was changing now. This wasn't what they'd expected. They'd expected a bunch of wee guys in casual gear who would run at the first sign of trouble. They were four years too late for that. Instead, what they had was two battle-hardened mobs who had spent the last four years knocking lumps out of each other, and who were relishing the chance to flex their muscles against a new opponent.

The battle edged its way up towards a load of red-blaes football pitches near Hampden. Bloody awful stuff that. Had Glasgow never heard of grass pitches? As the fighting continued we were enveloped in clouds of choking red dust as scuffling feet kicked up the blaes. You could tell the guys who'd been rolling around on the ground. Their clothes were covered in the stuff. By the time the coppers finally restored some order my lungs felt as if they were bursting. Mouthfuls of red dust did nothing for the breathing. Neither did battling your way up the road for the best part of two miles.

We expected that would be the end of it; we'd all get rounded up and chucked in the cells. Not a bit of it. The coppers restored our escorts and took us round to the old Celtic end at Hampden. We'd made sure we got tickets for that end because we knew that's where they would put the England fans. We were right and it was no guesswork. Two years earlier at the same fixture (23 May 1987) we'd been in that end and found ourselves next to a bunch of English. On the other side of them that day had been Aberdeen, quite by chance. This time it wasn't down to chance. It had been planned that way.

The cops marched the English fans down to the bottom of the old terracing there, right behind the goal. The cops were getting their own back by doing that. The view was terrible, and the cops knew it. So did we but we went down there regardless and split our mob. The two hundred Aberdeen went on one side of the English, the two hundred Hibs on the other.

The English clocked us and now they looked worried. They knew that not only were there thousands of growling bears behind them ready to kill them, but also they had four hundred game guys surrounding them. They did the bravado thing, starting up a chant of 'England, England' but within seconds a cry of 'CCS' had gone up, quickly followed by 'come on Aberdeen'. We were at it again but this time there was no room for manoeuvre. There were fans all around us as we battered into the English. The cops had no choice. They had to climb into the Celtic end and give them some protection and for the next ninety minutes we were subjected to a mind-numbing 0–0 draw.

At least we had the chance to recharge the batteries because one thing was for certain. It would be just as eventful on the way back into the city centre. It certainly was. England broke away from their police escort at Mount Florida train station and round – oh I'd lost count by then – started. They were ripping-up fences to use as weapons because the boys who'd been tooled up had been nicked by then. We went at them with fists and boots and it was chaos again. On Aikenhead Road, meanwhile, a breakaway group of English supporters were attacking ordinary Scotland fans making their way home. It was getting well out of control and all you could hear were sirens as police cars sped this way and that trying to quell the violence erupting across the south side of the city.

It would spread into the heart of Glasgow as the night went on. We had another battle on Jamaica Street bridge as we made our way back in town. By the time we reached Queen Street station, we were knackered and our numbers were well down. We'd had boys stabbed, slashed and nicked. Aberdeen were the same. There were far less of them going back up the road than came down.

Within twelve months we'd understand exactly how the English felt. In 1990 Scotland were the visitors to Wembley and we slipped our police escort and attacked a pub-load of English at Leicester Square. They turned out to be Chelsea crew and they weren't best pleased. As the pub emptied we realised we'd bitten off way more than we could chew. We didn't run but we got a right doing. Chewing was the last thing on our minds for a while after that.

But that day in Glasgow there was a total of 249 arrests, with six people taken to hospital suffering from slash wounds. Questions were asked in the House of Commons about the orgy of violence.

There were calls for the game to be scrapped altogether. And England fans got the blame for caving in the pub windows in Victoria Road. At least that was something. As our mob and Aberdeen's waited for our respective trains we agreed it had been a job well done. There was no back-slapping, not even a polite handshake.

Just a nod of acknowledgement and we were off home.*

Two days later we were back in Glasgow waiting outside the Sheriff Court for some of our boys to come out. Rangers and Celtic crews were also there. They were planning to batter and rob any English who were released that morning. Now that lacks class and it's also cowardly. We had seen neither hide nor hair of Rangers or Celtic on the day of the big battle. There were still suggestions Rangers had fought for the other side. Yet two days later there they were – vultures waiting to feed off the scraps.

Our boys filtered out one by one and we asked them if they'd encountered any English. They said there were a couple of boys from Derby due out next. There was no way we were leaving them to the mercy of Celtic and Rangers. When they emerged we told them we'd take through them to Edinburgh with us. They looked unsure

---

* Many Scottish newspapers attributed the lion's share of the blame for the mayhem to England fans. The *Sunday Mail* of 28 May 1989 was fairly typical, noting that: 'Yesterday we witnessed the ugly face of England's soccer hooligans.' The truth, however, was that the Scottish 'supermob' put together by the CCS was every bit as organised, and violent, as its counterparts from south of the border. Whoever was to blame it was undoubtedly one of the bloodiest battles in the annals of football hooliganism, despite the massive police presence. One resident of Queen's Park – who had witnessed many clashes between rival fans on their way to Hampden – said that Celtic–Rangers games were like a 'Sunday-school picnic compared to today'.

but we assured them that what had happened on Saturday stayed on Saturday. The poor sods were skint; the last of their cash had gone on fines. All they had were their train tickets.

We took them through to Edinburgh, got them a bite to eat and picked their brains about English mobs. It was the least they could tell us in return for a good feed. And they turned out to be right good lads. They came up to a couple of Hibs games with a few of their mob and we went down there. Who'd have thought people you were battering on a Saturday morning would be your bosom buddies by a Monday afternoon.

Hey, nobody said the world of the CCS made sense.

13

HIGHWAY TO HULL

The last thing you could expect as a Hibs fan was a glamour friendly. The pre-season fixtures in 1989 were against Hull, Burnley and Aston Villa. The three games were to be played in the space of a week and that was a no-no for a lot of the boys because they had jobs to hold down. Let's face it; you're not going to toss away a week's holiday to go to Hull and Burnley, are you?

I wasn't even certain most of us knew where the hell Burnley was. I certainly couldn't have picked it out on a map of Britain. It's fair to say enthusiasm for these games was not at its highest. In fact, it was so muted there were only fourteen of us planning to do all three games. That's when you get into dangerous territory because we were a known mob by then. There was no question we'd be sorely tested because we were so short-handed. At least most of the boys were planning to go to Birmingham for the Villa game. But until then it was to be an intrepid little band heading off for the not-so-bright spots of England.

We hired two Transit vans and chucked mattresses into the back of them. Nothing like travelling in style. And that was nothing like travelling in style but needs must when money was tight. Six or seven of us would travel in the back of each van, and that was also where we would sleep. We reckoned all three games would be tasty. Burnley had a known mob, Villa had a known mob and Hull's a dump. You tend to find that crap towns have decent mobs, I don't know why. Maybe it's because there's nothing else to do in these places.

Hull was the first stop for us and we headed down the M1 in the vans. We had been right about the place being a tip. It was horrible. Their ground, Boothferry Park, wasn't much better but once we'd parked the vans, we grabbed a bite to eat. Then it was off to the ground and we thought we may as well start as we meant to go on. We were going in blind because we hadn't even sussed out what size their mob was but, nevertheless, we paid our way into the Hull end. Just as well Newcastle weren't there. They'd have been cursing us. But that's what we did. We paid our way into the home end, all fourteen of us. We were as nutty as fruit bats.

As we were walking around the terracing we spotted this fat guy in a Hearts top, hurling abuse at the Hibs players and the wee knot of fans in the away end. He did for starters. As we walked past him one of the boys decked him with a peach of a punch and it kicked-off from there. It got the attention of their mob and some of their scarfers fancied a go as well. That was what we came for and we were battling before the game had even started. Who needed a huge mob? I saw some ugly big guy coming towards me who looked as though he'd stopped a few punches in his time. There was no backing down now and within a few seconds his face had stopped another punch because I caught him flush in the kisser. The big bugger never flinched and I thought 'Uh, oh'. Presumably his face was in that state because he led with it, but fortunately I didn't get to sample his punching power. The cops waded in and dragged us away from the angry mob. Bizarrely enough, they didn't even throw us out of the ground. They just marched us round to the 'Hibs' end and that was a laugh. By putting us in there they probably doubled our team's support.

That wasn't the most comfortable ninety minutes we'd spent in a football ground because we knew what was waiting for us. Their mob would be raging that we'd got in, decked a boy and got out again without them landing a serious blow. We reckoned we were in for a right doing when we left the ground. Suddenly, coming to Hull didn't seem such a great idea. But when we left the ground there were no Hull fans to be seen. For some reason they didn't even fancy it after the match. Maybe they were warned off by the cops. Maybe our reputation had preceded us. But whatever the cause, we didn't hang around to find out. We got in our vans and got on our way.

* * *

Hull had been a sobering experience because we knew for certain Burnley had a serious mob and we weren't going to have many more bodies. We called one of our guys in Edinburgh to tell him what had happened in Hull and he told us another six were coming down in a third Transit van for the Burnley match on the Wednesday. Six. That would take us up to twenty, which was still far too short-handed. We arranged a meeting point with them because they were travelling on the Tuesday and we didn't want to have to stay in Burnley overnight. One day would be plenty, thanks.

On the day of the game we parked up near the ground, just in case we had to make a quick getaway. Then we went for a wander around the town's pedestrian precinct and we spotted a pub. There's nothing like a pint to steady the nerves so we went in and parked ourselves at a table. If we were hoping to keep a low profile we couldn't have chosen a worse pub in which to do it. We didn't realise it but we were in the Burnley mob's pub. We were sitting there blissfully unaware that we'd landed slap-bang in the middle of enemy territory. How could we have known? We'd never been to Burnley before.

So we were sitting there having a drink during the day, all twenty of us, but we thought there was something strange about this boozer. People were coming into the place in twos and threes, taking a quick look at us, then leaving again without ordering a drink. They had sussed us but we hadn't really sussed them. As the day went on the word was obviously going around Burnley that not only were Hibs in town, but also we'd had the gall to go into their boozer and take it over. It wasn't really like that but it didn't matter either way. They reckoned we were taking the piss, we weren't about to dissuade them from that notion, so it was all going to kick-off. There was no chance that we would run but even if we had been thinking about it couldn't have happened. The longer we were in the pub, the more the twos and threes coming and checking us out became fours and fives.

When we finally looked out of the pub window there was a handy mob of them and they were motioning us to come out. We were happy to oblige. We flew out the door and got steamed in. By Christ those Burnley boys could fight. We were taking some big hits and coming back with our own and this was all going on in the pedestrian precinct. The weirdest thing was that there was a hotel right across the road from this pub and that was where the Hibs team was staying. The players were all hanging out of the windows watching the fight take place. What a role reversal. Instead of us watching them, they got to watch us in action for a change.

The coppers came and separated the warring factions, not a moment too soon because we were in danger of being overwhelmed. They gave us an escort to Turf Moor, Burnley's ground, and when we got inside we could see that only a handful of scarfers had made the trip. They actually looked quite pleased to see us because the Burnley fans in general aren't the most welcoming and they felt quite intimidated. You couldn't blame scarfers for not making the journey down. Wednesday night in Burnley doesn't exactly get the juices flowing, unless you were nutters like us.

As soon as we got inside the ground we did our usual and made for the segregation fence. There must have been about two hundred of the Burnley mob there by then and we stood at that fence singing 'You're gonna get your fucking heads kicked in.' We kept that up throughout the ninety minutes and they were getting seriously upset at these mouthy Jocks taking the piss inside their own ground. It was bravado, pure and simple, on our part.

At the end of the game we came out of the ground and walked down a wee lane. We turned left, went down to the bottom of the street and that's where they were waiting for us. The problem was that a line of police were in the way. Time for more bravado, or stupidity, or whatever you want to call it. We tried to break through the police lines and get at the Burnley mob, but, as we did so, some of them came up behind us through an alley. We spotted them and made a run towards them in the alley and started battling.

I wonder if those breakaways of theirs ever realised what they did. We were delighted to take on the splinter group instead of the main mob because it would have been carnage if we'd had to take on the whole two hundred. Instead, we twice fought Burnley to a standstill in their own town. The police waded in and stopped us battling once again and, as we looked down the street, we could see there were loads and loads of them, just itching to come up and give us a doing. But the coppers had a tight grip and they told us to get in our vans and get on our way. Nobody was arguing. It was the safest thing to do that night.

* * *

We had a couple of days to regroup until the clash with Aston Villa and we just bummed around Lancashire before driving down the M6 to get closer to Birmingham. By the way, the idea of chucking mattresses into the back of a Transit van and making some kind of poor man's caravan out of it wasn't the greatest brainwave. When six or seven blokes are on the road together they don't eat sensibly, they eat rubbish. And they drink pints. So when they're crashed out on their mattresses in their sleeping bags they fart. Quite a lot. The stench in those vans every morning would have made a glass-eye water. And no matter how long we left the back doors open, the perfume of the day was Eau de Fart.

Anyway, the Villa game was on the Saturday and we expected it to be the big one. Everybody was committed to going so we knew we'd have a good crew. There were eight or nine minibuses leaving from Edinburgh and they were meeting at Hilton Park services, the last big service station before you reach the Birmingham turn-off from the motorway. That was where we were meeting them as well.

The instruction to the boys driving down from Edinburgh was to avoid travelling in a convoy. They made their arrangements the night before and worked out who was going with whom. Then everyone would meet up at Hilton Park because there were other people coming down in cars and vans. From there we'd travel in convoy into Birmingham. We got to the service station and around 140 boys had turned up, a good number. Then it was wagons roll and we were off into Birmingham.

We'd heard Birmingham was a hard city so weren't going to be wandering around in separate groups, it was all for one and one for all. Did I say it was wagons roll? More like wagons stop. The motorway down to Birmingham was gridlocked. How can people live there with that traffic? All three lanes were stopped dead. The boys in the minibuses had their doors open, our Transit-van doors were open, and we were having a carry-on in the middle of the M6. Eventually, we got moving and we decided to park at the ice rink. The places we planned to go in Birmingham were the Bull Ring, because we figured there would be mobs hanging around there, and New Street train station, because we had some more boys coming down by rail. The ice rink was within striking distance of both those places.

Now, the one place you can be guaranteed to come across opposition fans is at a train station. Yet we never saw one at New Street, just our own boys. With the mob all together we went to the Bull Ring, figuring there would a bit of action on the go there. We were bound to chance upon some mob's pub. Nothing happened. Typical. We chanced upon Burnley's pub when there were twenty of us, but we couldn't find a mob's pub when we were team-handed. We walked to Villa Park, and that's no short distance. Still nothing. We were so sure they were bricking it that we even split up inside the ground, some of us going behind the goal, some of us going into the area reserved for Hibs fans. Still nothing.

After the match we came out into the street opposite the main stand and we were just waiting for everyone to link up again. No sooner had that happened than we spotted Villa for the first time all day. We went mental and tore at them and they didn't fancy it. They tried to stand and not lose face but we hadn't come all the way down to Birmingham to take home a second prize and we hammered them. They turned and ran. They actually ran back into the ground.

The police came racing into the fray and arrested a couple of our boys, my brother being one of them. They rounded us up and informed us we'd be escorted into the city centre, but we managed to escape the escort and legged it. The police were going crazy. The last thing they needed was a whole load of Hibs tearing about their city centre but we were gone. They needn't have worried. Villa were nowhere to be seen, and no other mobs came out to have a go.

We trooped back towards the ice rink thinking a lot less of Brummie mobs than we had before. But when we got back to the ice rink there was a group of guys standing outside and they obviously fancied themselves. They started mouthing off at us as we headed back to the vans. I didn't know if they were part of a mob or just arseholes but our guys fired the verbals straight back and pretty soon there were threats being made and people were squaring up. The next thing we knew, the ice-rink doors burst open and out charged an ice-hockey team complete with their big sticks and their padding on. We all stood there for a moment, because we couldn't believe our eyes. We'd fought plenty of football mobs in our time but an ice-hockey team? Well, what do you think?

But in for a penny, in for a pound, as they say. The battle started and it was just as well we had a big mob with us or we'd have been in trouble. Those ice-hockey sticks were serious weapons and these jokers swung them about as if they were determined to take our heads off. They probably fancied their chances when they came charging out that door but they must have been given a bum steer about how many of us there were. Either that or they were even nuttier than us. Whatever, they copped a hammering, both the ice-hockey team and the mouthy mob.

One of our guys was diabetic and he carried a syringe so he could take his insulin. He got one of the ice-hockey boys down on the ground and stabbed his needle into him two or three times. The bloke must have been crapping himself when he realised he'd been stabbed with a needle by a crew from Edinburgh, given our city's heroin problem. He'd have been thinking HIV, Aids, hepatitis. Take your pick; he'd have been certain our boy had one of them, coming from Edinburgh.

We routed the ice-hockey mob, we really did. There were a few battered bodies lying about that car park by the time we climbed back into our transport for the journey north. Not only were we Scotland's number-one soccer crew, but we'd also become ice-hockey's first casuals as well.

Now that's what you call branching out.

14

BEDLAM IN BELGIUM

European nights didn't come around too often for us so when Hibs were drawn against FC Liège in the UEFA Cup of 1989/90 everyone was well up for it. We got the train to London, then on to Dover and caught the ferry to Ostend. From there it was easy enough to get to Liège by train. I don't know about you but I'd always imagined Liège would be a nice place. It's not. It's a dump, a really industrial city. Still, we had about one hundred boys with us and we weren't there to admire the views. We were looking for a battle.

On the day of the game, 31 October 1989, we hung around Liège and there was no sign of any sort of mob on their side. There weren't too many coppers and we didn't even get an escort to the ground. But after the match it was a different story. The Hibs fans were kept in the ground until the home fans cleared. Then there was a heavy police presence as they walked us down the hill away from the stadium. As we looked down the road we could see a large group of guys standing at the entrance to a tunnel. We asked the coppers who they were and one policeman replied, 'You don't want to go near them. They are the hooligans of Liège.' He'd barely got the word 'Liège' out before we'd broken through our escort and were tearing down the road. The Belgians scattered in all directions, which was a disappointment. We'd thought that by showing out the way they had they were up for a battle. Maybe they hadn't expected us to make the first move. Maybe they were all show. We'd soon find out.

For all that they had scattered, they were still in three groups and we were gaining rapidly on one group. When we caught up with them they didn't want to know. If they could have put their hands up they would have but we weren't for stopping now. We were gasping and panting from the chase but we still laid into them.

The second group turned back to help their mates while the third had circled round some side streets and attacked us from behind. This was more like it, a good old battle, but the Belgians were fighting simply to survive. We were fighting out of choice and that gave us the edge. We were gaining the upper hand when the coppers arrived in their cars, sirens wailing. They didn't take any prisoners, laying into us with truncheons to get us away from their countrymen. In the end, they succeeded and they rounded us up and marched us off to the railway station. We might not have had an escort to the ground but they made sure we had one going back, not just to the railway station but all the way to Ostend.

It was only on board the ferry that we were finally rid of the police and the drink started to flow. Once we disembarked at Dover a few of the boys were the worse for wear and things were getting out of control. It was almost inevitable something would kick-off on the train to London and it did. One guy started ripping up the seats then one of the seats was lifted clean off its mountings and hurled through the window. It wasn't pretty. By the time the train reached London one carriage had been completely trashed.*

---

* A statement issued by British Transport Police at the time confirms Dykes's account of the journey: it described how fans hurled seats from train windows, smashed toilets and terrorised other passengers. But the trouble should not have come as a surprise to the authorities: the *Daily Record* reported that the CCS had been boasting for months of the mayhem it would cause when Hibs got back into Europe. AC

It was back to police escorts again. There was another load of coppers waiting for us when the train reached the station. They nicked eighteen of us and I was one of them. It didn't help that I had a warrant out for non-payment of a fine so we were all shipped off to Rochester Row police station and questioned through the night. We all stuck to the same story, claiming that we'd been sleeping and had no idea who'd smashed up the train. There were no witnesses, so there was no charge and everyone got out except me. They were going to keep me in because of the non-payment of the fine but the boys had a whip-round and paid what I owed. We were put on a train back to Edinburgh, oblivious to the fact that word of our exploits had been all over the television news back home.

The law was waiting for us in Edinburgh as well, wanting to ask us more questions and shake our story. It wasn't just coppers who were waiting either. There were a bunch of newspaper reporters and photographers and as we got shoved into the back of a van, the photographers were snapping away. The guy sitting next to me pushed his chest up against the van window, and pulled his shirt open to reveal the T-shirt he was wearing beneath it. It read, 'Capital City Service'. And the following morning, it was on the front page of every newspaper.**

* * *

You would think that having sampled the Capital City Service once, the Belgian coppers would have put a stop to us travelling to their country again. Not a bit of it. When Hibs were drawn to face

---

** The *Daily Record* was one of the papers to carry the image on its front page. It is reproduced on the first page of the illustrations in this book. AC

Anderlecht in the 1992/93 UEFA Cup, our passports were looked out again. The plan was to get the train down to London then head on to Brussels for the game, which was to be played on 29 September 1992. The trip didn't start well. Two Hibs fans fell off the Edinburgh to London train on the way down and were killed. Then word reached us that some Hibs scarfers who had decided to go to Brussels via Amsterdam were being terrorised by the Rangers mob.

Rangers had a European tie in Denmark, against Lyngby, the same week and a few of their cavemen were breaking the journey in Amsterdam. From what we were told they saw the Hibs scarfers as an easy target and had set about them in Amsterdam's red-light district. Now that's just not on. The one thing the Capital City Service never did was take liberties and that was taking liberties. The Rangers scarfers had vastly superior numbers in Amsterdam and were just bullying our scarfers. We weren't going to let that happen. So it meant a change of plan and a wee diversion to Amsterdam to put matters straight.

Some of our mob had planned on flying to Amsterdam before going to Brussels anyway so we knew would have a decent number available to dispense justice. As soon as we reached Amsterdam we booked ourselves into a hostel and waited for night time before heading into the red-light district to deal with Rangers. And once we were out and about, the word got around pretty quickly that we were in town. Suddenly, they weren't so brave. Suddenly, Hibs scarfers were able to enjoy the delights of the red-light district without being jumped by Rangers. And when we finally did have a coming together, they really didn't cover themselves in glory. By the 1990s the Capital City Service were known all over Scotland and the big-shot Rangers fans who thought they were running the show in Amsterdam were shiting themselves at the prospect of facing us. It showed, because as soon as they bumped into us, or should I say as soon as we hunted them down, they weren't much for fighting.

Our violence was fuelled by anger and we weren't holding back. There were no weapons involved, just fists and feet, but we gave them one hell of a hiding. My abiding memory of that night is of one Rangers fan being so petrified when the fighting started that he dived into a canal to get away from us. We were on one of the little bridges that spanned this particular canal, the whole mob of us baying and jeering at this pathetic wee guy as he tried to swim to safety. I tell you what; he had more to fear from the water in that canal than he did from us. We'd have given him a kicking and let him hobble off to lick his wounds. If he swallowed any of that canal water, he'd have been risking life and limb licking his fingers.

It was one of those great moments as a mob, standing on that little bridge. We were one unit, we'd stood while the opposition had run and we were on the high you always get after a victory like that. We headed off to one of the local pubs to bask in our glory and celebrate with a few pints of Dutch beer. I don't know what time we got back to the hostel but it was late. I don't know what time the banging started on the door of our room but it was early. And when we opened the door there was a posse of riot cops outside. They weren't messing about either. Word had reached them about the previous night's battle in the red-light district and they'd come to run us out of town.

Showering wasn't an option. The message was simple. The train leaves for Brussels from Centraal station in half an hour. Be on it. Missing the train wasn't an option either because it was made crystal clear that if we weren't on that train, we'd be in a cell. So once again we had a guard of honour. This time it wasn't Scottish coppers but Dutch riot police and, with their guns and riot shields, they didn't look like blokes to take liberties with. They took us all the way to Centraal station and even waited on the platform until the train had pulled out of the station, just to make sure we didn't hop off the train. They needn't have worried. We had an appointment in Brussels and a battle planned with the Anderlecht mob.

As soon as we reached Brussels we split up and made our way to the various hotels and hostels we'd booked into. We arranged to meet up back at the train station and head for the red-light district in Brussels. A few local skinheads were giving us gyp there and we battered them, pure and simple. Then some of the Anderlecht mob appeared and there were skirmishes, no more than that, but we stood and they ran.

We found a pub with open-air tables and some of us were inside the pub and some of us outside. It made no difference because when the cops arrived they grabbed the lot of us. I was sitting inside when a big copper walked in with the blond hair and moustache, looking every inch a porn star. He whacked me across the face with a rubber truncheon and I said to my mate, 'Is my nose broken?' Then he whacked me again, right across the bridge of the nose. I didn't need to ask a second time. There was blood everywhere. These guys weren't messing about.

They rounded up seventy-five CCS and took us to the police station, where we were told to empty our pockets. It was a rule with our guys that you didn't carry your passport when you were out because we figured if we got lifted they wouldn't deport you without it and it worked again. We were banged up in a cell for the night then, unbelievably, they let us out on the morning of the game. We were astonished. We felt certain our chance of seeing the match had gone because there was no way the cops would let us anywhere near it.

Instead, we were waved on our way so we arranged to meet at lunchtime in the Grand Platz in Brussels, a beautiful big square right in the heart of the city. When we got there it was alive with

Hibs fans; there were about a thousand of them plus a hundred of our mob. Everyone was just enjoying a few beers and it was all pretty good natured. There were some Arabs hanging around trying to stir things up but we chased them off and we were all having a right good laugh during the afternoon. Then, about five o'clock, we decided to get the metro to the ground. While we were on the tube someone had the idea of getting off at the Arab quarter of Brussels; don't ask me whose idea it was or why he thought of it because I just don't know. It was that all for one, one for all, thing. Once one decided we all went.

The Arab quarter is quite sizeable in Brussels but the streets are very narrow. We were getting some suspicious looks from the local shopkeepers because we stuck out like a sore thumb and, naturally, after an afternoon's drinking, one or two of the boys were the worse for wear. Next thing we knew, one of them had staggered into a display outside one of the shops and the atmosphere changed in a heartbeat. Now it was no longer suspicion, it was aggression. The Arabs were furious that a display had been knocked over and people were appearing at every shop doorway. We just kept walking, but, from out of nowhere, a guy emerged with a big Stanley knife. He came right up behind Andy Tait and slashed him across the throat. That was the cue for it to kick-off big style. A battle started between the Arab shopkeepers and their pals and us, and it was mayhem.

My problem was that I had more to worry about than fighting right then because the blood was pumping out of Andy's throat and neck. Me and another two boys got a hold of him and wrapped a scarf tightly round his neck in an attempt to stem the flow of blood. The battle was raging but we had to try and get Andy away from it because his throat had been slit wide open. We were begging him to hang on but you could see the colour draining out of him; it was as if his life was ebbing away.

146

The problem was that more Arabs were coming to join the fight and they were armed to the teeth. They had everything but the kitchen sink with them. As we desperately looked around for an escape route we saw this wee street off to one side and there was an old woman standing in her doorway. She motioned for us to come over and we dragged Andy to her house and sat him down, propped up against the wall, in the street outside. He was still losing blood way too quickly so we tied another scarf around his neck but just as we were doing that the first of our mob came tearing past us. The arrival of Arab reinforcements had tipped the balance too heavily against us and it would have been suicide to fight a mob armed with machetes and some of the biggest knives I've ever seen. The old woman obviously realised Andy was in no shape to run and dragged him inside her house. Then she shut the door, leaving us outside in the street facing the angry mob.

Our first priority was to catch the rest of our boys and when you've got a baying mob looking to hack you to pieces, believe me you run fast. We could see the sign for the metro but they were gaining on us fast and we kicked over a couple of rubbish bins as we ran to try and slow them down. My heart was pounding and I'm not sure if it was fear of being caught by the mob or running flat out that was causing it. Probably a bit of both.

We belted down on to the metro platform where there were normal people going about their everyday business. As soon as we came careering in they scattered and we wound up battling with the first of the Arabs. At least when we reached the platform some of the boys were there to help us and we managed to hold them off long enough for a tube to arrive. We backed our way into a carriage while still swinging to stop the Arabs following us. It seemed to take an eternity for the doors to close but they finally did. The Arabs were furious. They were booting the side of the train and cursing us and we responded with jeers and V-signs because we were finally safe. As the train pulled out of the station we all looked at each other and laughed the sort of nervous laugh that doesn't really mask the fact you were shiting yourself.

That was one of the scariest incidents the CCS were ever involved in but, as usual, it didn't take us long to move on. As we made our way to Anderlecht's ground we came across the pub where their mob hung out. There was a load of them in there but they wouldn't come out and face us. I don't know if they'd clocked the size of our crew and decided they just didn't want to know, but they refused point blank to leave the pub. We were outside giving it big licks when the cops appeared, I assumed called by the publican. I couldn't work out what was going on at first. There was a hand sticking out of a police-car window holding what looked like a fire extinguisher but then they started spraying it and it was tear gas. People were scattering in all directions until a voice said in perfect English: 'Just stand by me lads and you'll be fine.' About twenty of the guys went towards him but it seemed too good to be true. Turned out he was an Edinburgh CID copper who'd been brought over from Scotland to keep tabs on us in Brussels. It must have been him who alerted his Brussels buddies it was all about to kick-off. The guys who'd stood beside him were immediately handed over to the police. But a load of us hadn't fallen for it and we legged it. The boys who stood beside the copper got deported. So much for the passport theory.

The rest of us went to the match and suddenly Anderlecht were feeling brave with a fence between us and them. They were less cocky when we started charging at the fence and climbing it. A few of us were tearing at the wire mesh with our bare hands and we actually managed to tear away the top of the fencing and coil it back. At one stage, we really fancied our chances of ripping the fence down and getting at Anderlecht and they weren't feeling so brave once they spotted that happening. Unfortunately, the cops also spotted what we were up to and they came wading in, batons swinging. We briefly battled with them but as reinforcements arrived we backed off sharpish. I, for one, was glad about that. My nose couldn't take any more.

During the match Anderlecht started giving it big licks again, figuring they were now safe. They weren't. Our mob started ripping up the seats and tossing them over the fence. Cue another battle with the coppers. Cue another tactical retreat by us. I think the cops just couldn't wait for the game to end and, when it did, Hibs were out of Europe again. But we still had the rest of the night in Brussels and it was back to the Grand Platz for more beer. It was far more dangerous this time. The Arabs had mobilised and they spent hours charging at us in the square. We stood firm and saw them off but the coppers were in and out of the square half the night.

By the time things had calmed down a few of the boys decided to go on the rob. It was a practice started by Liverpool's casuals. Essentially, why buy good gear when you can nick it? We found a few decent shops, their windows got caved in and we helped ourselves to top-of-the-range gear. One of our mob clearly didn't understand how it worked, though. The idea was that you lifted something that was easily concealed inside your jacket so that, when the coppers came, there was nothing obviously untoward about you. He spotted a leather jacket he fancied but when the cops showed up he was the first one to be chased. He was walking down the street with the leather jacket still around the tailor's dummy, which was tucked under his arm!

The following day we got the train to Ostend to catch a ferry back to Dover and we still had no word about how Andy was. We couldn't even risk going to the hospital to find out, because we'd have been nicked for certain. But when we got to the ferry port at Ostend the police were all lined up to make sure we left without causing any trouble and they were gleefully telling us, 'Your friend is dead.'

The atmosphere was pretty grim on the boat as we mulled over the news and by the time we reached Dover and got on a train to London we were drunk and ready for trouble. Thankfully, given our previous actions on a boat train, people did just fall asleep this time. If we'd trashed another train we'd have been doing time in a London prison. It was only when we got home that we learned the Belgian police had lied to us. Andy was still alive. He was forced to spend a week in hospital and it was touch and go for a couple of days. That was to prove the last of his adventures with us.

We couldn't blame him.

15

PROPAGANDA WAR

By the late 1980s I think the coppers were at their wits' end with us. No matter how much they tried to take control of the situation on match days, we were still running riot. That's when a new, and altogether more sinister, way of dealing with us surfaced. Stories started appearing in both the local Edinburgh newspapers and in the national press about us. Don't get me wrong. We didn't mind being featured in newspapers if it was reports of our battles. We kept all those cuttings because they were almost like badges of honour. The more the newspapers wrote about you, the more successful you were at what you were doing. I don't know a casual who didn't keep the cuttings about his crew. Most of the boys have scrapbooks or bags of cuttings to this day, although they're kept well out of the way of the kids.

But cuttings about battles were one thing. Some of the rubbish that was being written in the late Eighties and early Nineties was another. It was almost as if there was a concerted campaign between the coppers and their pals in the newspapers to demonise us. A whole series of articles appeared in which the Capital City Service was getting blamed for virtually every crime that took place in

Edinburgh. If someone got assaulted on a Sunday night somewhere in Edinburgh, the papers would report police as saying they believed it was the work of the CCS. If the assailants happened to say 'We are Hibs' that apparently proved it; CCS to blame again. Never, in all the time I was battling, did I say 'We are Hibs' and neither did any of the guys I was fighting alongside.

There was one particularly nasty assault in Edinburgh in which the attackers were reported as having spoken those words, and the police were quoted as saying they believed it to be the work of Hibs casuals. The phone lines between our houses were red hot. CCS guys were ringing each other asking if they'd been battling that night and not one of them knew anything about it.

If the coppers were looking to unsettle us they weren't succeeding but they had other tricks up their sleeve. A journalist who had written an 'exclusive' insight into the world of the Capital City Service for his newspaper had apparently seen the police dossiers on us. And these dossiers revealed we were running protection rackets. Apparently we were telling publicans that if they didn't employ our guys as bouncers, we'd come in and smash up their pubs. I can just imagine telling our guys they'd have to work as doormen at boozers. They'd have lasted five minutes. First hint of trouble they'd have waded in, given the miscreant a good doing and walked away from the job.

No wonder the coppers couldn't catch us back then. They were looking for us standing outside pubs, and we were all inside enjoying a pint. The problem was that we were becoming so well known in Edinburgh, or notorious if you like, that copycat gangs were springing up all over the place. We called them chippie casuals, because that's what they were. They hung around chip shops or corner shops. They were bunches of wee neds who wore the gear but picked on anyone and everyone and that just wasn't our style. We kept to football-related matters, the chippie casuals ran around causing mayhem. They weren't casuals at all, not in our sense of the word anyway. But the more they got up to, the more we got the blame.

It was bad enough being accused of demanding protection money and of randomly picking fights. Then the race card was played. An Asian shopkeeper in the Dumbiedykes area of Edinburgh had graffiti sprayed on the shutters of his store. It was the usual knuckle-draggers' stuff: 'Go home scum'; 'No blacks allowed'; 'Take your tribe home'; 'Your van's next'. A knife had been painted on the pavement with the words 'I wonder' alongside it. Swastikas and National Front symbols had also been daubed. And, very helpfully, 'CCS' and 'Hibs on tour in Scotland' had been added.

The report in the *Edinburgh Evening News* noted that: 'There have been recent claims that the football casuals are involved with extreme right-wing groups and it is thought some Hibs casuals have recently taken to wearing South African rugby jerseys.' This was all supposed to have taken place in the early hours of a Sunday morning, when any CCS I know would have been asleep, having been out most of Saturday between the football and the pub at night. But it served to demonise us even further, at a time when the public were being asked to grass us up if they saw us. That was what it had come to.

In the *Edinburgh Evening News* of 13 October 1990, an article appeared:

> Police today called for public help in an effort to beat the casuals problem. They called on anyone with information about casuals to contact them. But they rejected claims they were trying to sweep the problem under the carpet.
>
> They also spelled out their response in dealing with the casuals problem in the Lothians. They said they were well aware of the alleged activities of people masquerading under the casual banner.
>
> Police also said they were aware of the shoplifting

activities of the Hibs Baby Crew, but had been unable to attribute any particular case to any group or organisation, that information received by Lothian and Borders Police regarding spectators travelling to Millwall was passed to the appropriate force in London, that inquiries were still continuing into incidents at Easter Road games and that the plan by casuals for a winter of violence was well known.

In other words, the coppers were coming under pressure and they hadn't a clue how to stop us. Or rather, this was their way – make us out to be the Mafia in another guise and hope it would work. It didn't. The public was no more inclined to turn us in than they had been in the past. They didn't want to know because we weren't bothering them.

Then the coppers played another card. A leaked CID report linked the CCS to two murders. Detective Inspector John Gunderson's report, leaked to *The Sun*, said:

> At least two murders, and other serious attacks, can be laid fairly and squarely at the feet of Hibs Casuals. Numerous arrests have been made on their number but as yet it has not deterred them. The gang's morale has been lifted by cases being marked No Proceedings and when they realise the courts are not sentencing offenders heavily. If these people cannot cause trouble at a football match, then they will head to the city centre to cause trouble there.

He was right on one point but wrong on three. Yes, two people who at one time had run with the CCS had been convicted of murder. But these incidents were nothing to do with us; they weren't football-related. It was the equivalent of a copper getting done for murder while he was off duty and the headline reading 'Lothian and Borders Police linked to murder'.

Gunderson was right that we weren't worried about getting lifted because the normal penalty was a slap on the wrist. But the only time we headed into the city centre to cause trouble after a match was when the rival mob was going to be there. And being arrested was no deterrent. As I said, the plan was to demonise us and, while some people might have bought it, thankfully others didn't. The cops and the newspapers were desperate to put us in the worst possible light for one simple reason. They had underestimated the CCS, and casuals in general, from the off. At the time casuals came into being in Scotland, the image of the football hooligan was still that of the bovver boy. You know the script. Doc Marten boots, jeans and braces, skinhead haircut, denim jacket. We came along and the cops dismissed us as a passing fad. To be fair, even the more traditional football hooligans did that, until they got their first kicking from us.

But because the cops hadn't taken us seriously, they were miles behind when they suddenly decided they had to catch up. Bear in mind there were very few all-ticket matches back then. The Hillsborough disaster only happened in the late Eighties and it, and the Taylor Report that followed, were the catalysts for all-seater stadia. Before then it was standing on the terraces and clubs were happy to cram in as many folk as they could. You could pay into the ground anywhere you wanted and we made hay while the sun shone. Going into the opposition end was the quickest way to start a fight.

I suppose the cops figured we'd soon get sick of battling against the odds but they were wrong. That was part of the buzz. As one year of casual violence became two, then three, four and five, the cops tumbled to the fact that this wasn't going away. If anything, it was getting worse and people were getting sick of the lack of arrests. The cops might have denied they were sweeping it under the carpet but that's exactly what they were doing. They were writing it off as a bad two hours on a Saturday and dumping people back on trains.

I've already mentioned that I got nicked and let go when they collared an Aberdeen fan in my place. That wasn't the only time it happened. During a night game at Easter Road I got grabbed for battling. As the copper went to put me in the van I explained to him that I hadn't parked my car properly because the battle had started right in front of me and I'd got out of my car and waded in. I asked if I could at least park my car up before I got nicked and he agreed and let me walk away to do that. I didn't even drive at the time.

The coppers had no idea how to regain control of the situation and they were getting stick from all sides. Edinburgh publicans were sick of being caught in the thick of it and demanded action. Clothes-shop owners claimed the Baby Crew were descending in their droves and shoplifting whatever they needed to look good. They probably did because that was something first introduced into the casual way by Liverpool's mob.

But it wasn't just the coppers who had been remiss. The newspapers helped create the monster as well. They were happy enough to fill space with our 'wrongdoings' every day. There wasn't a Monday went by at the height of our battling without the local papers having another article about Hibs casuals running riot. It filled space for them. It filled our scrapbooks. It helped give us a name.

But by the end of the Eighties it became clear to our local papers that they had to do more than simply report what was going on. They started running articles about casuals themselves, rather than their exploits. At first we were happy about that. It gave us the chance to have our voice heard, to reassure the public that we weren't a danger to them. But the articles were so slanted that, in among the nice things they said about us, words like thug or phrases like 'bloodthirsty gang member' kept cropping up.

We'd been honest, we'd taken a chance on going to meet reporters and they were still selling us short. There was nothing else for it. Instead of setting up cloak-and-dagger meetings with the press we'd play the coppers at their own game. We'd send our boys to the newspaper offices and see if they'd have the balls to publish what we had to say. To be fair to the *Edinburgh Evening News*, they listened. And they published this article:

Six front-liners from Hibs Casuals who call themselves The Family came to the *News* office intent on clearing their names. All were young men, 20 and 21 years of age, presentable, polite, passionately proud of their team – a group of ordinary looking, casually dressed persons.

They could have been the answer to a recruiting sergeant's prayer – in times past. Today, however, they are a major headache for the police, who have to try to contain and seek to cool their almost ritualistic pitched battles with rival casuals before and after games.

However, what is more worrying is a new menace, gangs of youngsters styling themselves casuals who wander the streets looking for young teenagers, usually school-children on their way home from youth clubs and Scouts and Guide meetings, to corner and beat up.

This sinister new form of street violence was revealed in the *News* last week and concerns us greatly. Later, we were to find that true football casuals condemn what is happening in the streets just as vehemently as ourselves.

And they tell us why . . .

Hibs casuals admit to being football hooligans liking nothing better than a Saturday afternoon punch-up with casuals from rival football teams. But they insist that is the limit of their trouble-making.

They also insist that they have no connection to those

gangs who ape them and indeed dismiss them as the chippie casuals because of their habit of forming up around chip shops, especially in housing schemes.

'We don't go in for mindless violence and we want the public to know this and that they have absolutely nothing to fear from The Family and that is for sure,' says Peter, one of the front-liners.

'Those young idiots know we just don't want to know them. We don't want to be linked with these stupid, indiscriminate attacks on innocent kids. They are just getting us a bad name.'

Tony has £110 of one fine to pay for causing a breach of the peace at a recent Hibs match then he will start on instalments on another for £225, but he is jealous of the reputation of The Family and does not want to see it besmirched by the activities of other city gangs.

He explains: 'We are all football fanatics and we go to the games primarily because of this. To us, what happens on the field is just as important as what happens just before or just after the game. From Sunday to Friday we live football and on Saturday we fight football. We cannot fight in the grounds any more, because of the cameras they have installed, so we have to try and meet up with the rival casuals in the area around the grounds. Remember, we don't give trouble to the ordinary supporter of any team – only to the people who are out looking for a fight, people like ourselves and our own age group. The guys with the scarves we ignore, also the guy with a youngster or the guy with his bird. Being beaten up in front of your bird is dead humiliating so we don't do that to anyone.'

Three of the six who came to defend the name of The

Family have spent time in prison for persistent troublemaking. One had lost his home, two others their jobs and between them there were scar marks, a few once-fractured noses and the odd split knuckle.

It was a price they accepted to defend the name of The Family as the great fighting force in Premier League football.

But why do intelligent young adults like them want to battle every Saturday there is a Premier League match being played?

Alex, who has been a Hibs casual for four years, undertook to answer. 'Three or four years ago, there were only 30 or 40 casuals at Easter Road. We used to get pushed around with the ordinary fans so we decided it was time to give Hibs fans a bit of their pride back. This is vitally important, certainly to us.'

God knows what the cops thought of that article when they saw it. They were probably raging with the *Edinburgh Evening News*. Their charm offensive with the papers had come back and bitten them on the bum because we had humanised ourselves in the pages of the very same newspaper they'd used.

For all we knew, most ordinary folk could have read that and thought we were a bunch of tossers. The point of it wasn't to make ourselves liked. It was to prove to ordinary folk that we weren't running around battering kids, or daubing racist graffiti on Asian shops, or murdering people. Yes, we were having battles at the football and if the papers wanted to write that about us, fair enough. But to suggest the CCS were being run like some sort of private army was reprehensible and we weren't going to let that one go unchallenged. Our mini charm offensive might not have achieved much, but at least it let people know we weren't the monsters the coppers would have them believe.

The stupid headlines just kept on coming. It made the news that a Hibs casuals football team had been kicked out of an amateur league, for fear of violence. Big deal. Teams get kicked out of amateur leagues every week. Just because this team was seen as being 'our' team, it became a national story. Honest to God, if it rained in Edinburgh they thought about blaming us for it. Still, I suppose we couldn't have it both ways. We wanted them to write football-violence-related stories and you could argue that was one. It beat the hell out of being branded a bunch of drug-pushing Godfathers by the coppers.

To this day, casuals are still big news. Any hint of an upsurge in violence and the papers are full of it. The Casuals Are Back. Return of the Casuals. New Casuals Fear. You want to know the truth? They never went away. The mobs may have diminished over the years and you may have stopped reading about them. That was probably because the cops didn't need the papers as casual numbers went down. And when we weren't in the papers it was out of sight, out of mind.

The cops had swept it back under the carpet.

16

THE LIONS' DEN

'We thought Edinburgh was civilised compared to the Glasgow teams. We never expected anything like this. Millwall supporters have had a bad name over the years but this is the worst I have ever seen.'

Greig Tarrant, landlord, Crown and Anchor pub,
New Cross, London

Ever had your Christmas and birthday presents rolled into one? The CCS did back in 1990 when Hibs' pre-season fixtures were announced. As we scanned the list of games to see what trips and battles awaited us, one fixture couldn't have stood out more clearly if it had been surrounded by flashing neon lights. There was a Friday-night friendly, away at Millwall.

Millwall, for God's sake.

We were practically dancing in the streets. If ever a mob's reputation preceded them it was Millwall's. They were reckoned to be the hardest around and to take them on in their own back yard was a chance we couldn't have dreamed of. The planning began almost immediately. Those wanting to make the trip had to submit their names and deposits were collected. We needed to know in advance how many were going so that we could be certain we had enough bodies to handle what was coming. This wasn't an away day in Glasgow or Aberdeen where you took your chances with however many of you there were. This was Millwall at The Den. Christ, even the name of the ground is intimidating.

But we were fortunate that a couple of our mob were based in London so doing a recce of the area wasn't a problem. When you're going to a place like Millwall everything needs to be planned. We had to know where their pub was, how we'd travel there, how far it was to the ground from there, what the layout of the area was. Being ambushed by two hundred of the Millwall mob was not going to be on the agenda. We had to make the first move.

There was also the small matter of letting them know we were coming and we needed the name of their boozer to give them a call. As it turned out, we got a lucky break. One of our London boys got the tube to New Cross to check out the area and was collared by a copper the minute he left the station. He thought he was one of the Birmingham crew who had come to check things out and asked where he was from. As soon as our guy said 'Scotland', he was allowed to go on his way.

So we had the layout of the area, we'd let Millwall know we were coming and everything was set. It's amazing how fearless you are when you're young. I don't think any of us ever considered just how badly wrong this could go. All we cared about was the fact we were going to take on Millwall. To us this was the crème de la crème, the heavyweight championship of the world. In the week leading up to the game the excitement was building second by second. You could almost touch it. Any time you met a member of the CCS he had a smile on his face that no amount of bad news could have wiped off.

I had been in charge of collecting names, taking deposits and booking buses, along with another guy, and we were going to have a strong mob. We soon had two hundred names on the list and the plan was to leave from the Royal Nip pub in Easter Road, just round the corner from Hibs' ground, at midnight on the Thursday. We booked three buses to ferry us down. On the day we were due to leave I packed a change of clothes in a bag. I stuck a decent amount of money in my pocket in case I needed to be bailed at any point, and, at the last minute, wrapped a small claw hammer in a plastic bag and stuck it in my holdall. I never, ever went tooled up to matches. It wasn't something the CCS really did. But this was Millwall, so my brother did the same.

As we made our way to the Royal Nip, we wondered how many people would actually turn up. We needn't have worried. The pub was so crammed we could barely get in the door. There must have been 250 guys wanting to make the trip. The atmosphere was electric. You could have lit up half of Edinburgh with the energy being generated. Blokes who had paid up had brought mates with them, who also fancied taking on the hardest crew of all. It was obvious there was going to be too many people for the number of buses we had booked but we figured we'd cram them all in somehow.

And then the police played their trump card. As soon as the buses turned up at the Royal Nip, the coppers appeared and ordered the drivers to take them away again. We were left high and dry without transport. The choice was simple. Put it down to bad luck and head up the town for a night-out or do our damnedest to get to London by any and every means. Most folk were of the same mind. We weren't going to pass up this chance. Plan B swung into action and it was planes, trains and automobiles. Some of our mob had access to a minibus and my brother and I managed to get into that. Others went by car. Some more got the morning train. Some caught the bus. A couple of guys even flew down. The bottom line was that instead of arriving as a mob that was two-hundred-strong, or more, we would be arriving in dribs and drabs. What made it even worse was that our meeting point was Shakes in London's Victoria, which was Chelsea's pub. Well, why not? If you're going to take on one top mob, why not have two for the price of one? As I said, when you're young you're fearless.

Now we were facing the prospect of being taken apart by Chelsea before we'd even got to Millwall. And just when it looked as though everything that could go wrong had gone wrong the coppers struck again. Our minibus was stopped as we were leaving Edinburgh. The police searched the bags and turned up the two claw hammers and other bits and bobs. It seemed some of the other boys had the same idea as us. The coppers asked who the bags belonged to and none of us piped up so they confiscated the lot. Then they checked our names and it turned out I had an unpaid fine so I had to fork out for that. That was my cash gone. It meant a detour back to the house to pick up a change of clothes and some more money before we finally set off. And our house was right out of claw hammers by then.

In an effort to make up for lost time, stops were kept to a minimum on the way down. But while the minibus was being filled up with petrol, I nipped into a service station to grab a can of deodorant because I'd forgotten to lift one from home. I stuck the can of Lynx in my pocket and we were back on the road again.

By the time we got to London and headed to Shakes a good idea suddenly didn't seem so good. We got into the pub to find that we were the first CCS there. Fortunately, Chelsea hadn't fronted up or it would have been a suicide mission. But as the minutes ticked by, with no sign of anyone else appearing, London was starting to feel like a very lonely place.

Then the doors opened and in walked a few of our crew. Then a few more. Then another group. There was a mixture of relief and anticipation as we downed a couple of pints before moving on to another meeting point to catch up with some more of our guys.

This time it was the Hog in the Pound, just off Oxford Street, and the boys were there. It was looking good. There were over a hundred of us and that was a good-enough mob to be going on with. Another couple of drinks and we were ready for action. Nobody was getting bevvied or anything like that. You're no use to anyone in a battle if you're tanked up and, in a battle like the one ahead, we all had to rely on each other.

Our recce guy had told us the best way to Millwall's pub was to catch the tube to New Cross, just as he'd done, so we headed off for the station. The hardest part was keeping a lid on the excitement because we were wired to the moon by then. I'd never known our mob so hyped-up but we had to keep it calm, because you draw enough attention to yourselves just by being on the move as a hundred-strong mob without doing anything else to get the coppers interested. No one wanted to get nicked before we'd even got to New Cross.

Once we got off the tube we came streaming out of the station and saw a couple of coppers on the other side of the road. The look on their faces was priceless. They couldn't believe their eyes when they realised how many of us had arrived as a mob. You know, most people who visit London will do a bit of sightseeing, visit the Tower of London, check out Buckingham Palace, maybe take in a show. Not us. We were the show and we were topping the bill on the Old Kent Road, which to most of us had only been a two-bob property on a Monopoly board until then.

The blood was pumping now. Here we were, walking down that very Old Kent Road, chanting our songs, ready to face Millwall.

Don't let anyone kid you there are no nerves at that point. Your stomach is in a knot, your palms are sweaty; the perspiration is trickling down your forehead. But I was secure in the knowledge that every guy around me was a fully fledged loony. These guys hadn't taken the easy option when the coppers sent our buses away. They'd stuck with it and done whatever it took to get here.

Then we spotted the Crown and Anchor. It wasn't difficult really because two huge Millwall buggers had come charging out of it. I ran straight at the first one and we went at it. I got a hold of him but he was so big I could barely get my arms round him. I was hitting him with everything I had and he was giving it back to me with interest. We were rolling about on the ground with me thinking 'I'm not doing so well here', when something sharp dug into my back. That bloody can of Lynx I'd bought at the service station! I reached into my pocket, pulled it out and held it in front of his face as if it was gas or mace. He wasn't to know it would only have made him the sweetest-smelling Millwall fan of all time and he loosened his grip enough for me to get free of him and rejoin the boys.

They were playing a blinder. It was absolute mayhem. Some Millwall guys had come out on to the street and were battling but the boys had backed them up to the door so the rest couldn't get out. A huge plant pot had been heaved through the pub window and other boys were ripping-up fencing to use the planks as weapons and setting about the Millwall mob. There were shouts and screams and curses and, to top it all, a car got overturned. Its alarm going off just added to the cacophony of noise. It was superb, absolutely superb, and it went on for at least five minutes before the coppers turned up. A few of the boys got nicked while they rounded up the rest of our mob and shunted us down a side street full of little terraced houses. The curtains were twitching as people peered out nervously from their windows to see what on earth was going on.

Then the ground came into view and it was just as intimidating as you'd expect. You went down a lane and through a tunnel and there you were. The Den. Before we could even get into the ground a load of Millwall's mob pitched up looking for revenge. Word had got out about what had happened to their pub and they were raging. They had been embarrassed on their own patch and they were hell-bent on revenge. These guys were no youngsters either. They would have been about forty if they were a day and they were big boys. They gave it the charge and we charged right back. It was brutal stuff but we gave as good as we got and we stood them, we didn't run. We took them on and even an undercover Edinburgh CID guy who was by then in our midst keeping tabs on us got caught up in it. He had to take a swing himself just to survive before the coppers came and broke it up. Millwall had been humiliated on their own patch for the second time in less than half an hour.

With the battling over I went to the turnstile to pay my way in. The coppers were searching everyone before they could even join the queue and as I was being patted down the cop found the can of Lynx in my pocket. 'What's this?' he asked. 'A can of deodorant,' I replied. And he nicked me for possession of an offensive weapon. Now I know Lynx might not smell too hot but it's pushing it to call it an offensive weapon. But he wasn't for listening and I got banged up for the night at the police station.

It sounded like I missed a lot of fun inside the ground. The boys were singing 'We thought you were hard, we were wrong,' which had the Millwall mob hopping up and down in fury on the other side of the fence. They were apparently telling the boys in great detail what was going to happen to them after the game and it wasn't pretty. The only problem for Millwall was that there were coppers by the vanload waiting outside the ground to escort our guys to the station afterwards and Millwall couldn't get near them.

A couple of our real nutters even tried to break the police lines to get at the rival mob.

The boys spent the rest of the night roaming around London trying to find another mob to fight because they were so pumped up by the Millwall experience. They reckoned they might run into Arsenal or Spurs around Victoria or Euston, because they had been playing friendlies that night as well. They were popping in and out of tube stations like meerkats on speed but they drew a blank.

I, meanwhile, was taken from my cell the following morning to go to court. Saturday court, can you believe it? I expected to see the other Hibs boys who had been nicked but there was just me. When I asked the police where my mates were I was told they'd all been released the same night because their charge was one of mobbing and rioting and they'd agreed to appear in court later that week. I was being charged with possession of an offensive weapon and I pleaded guilty just to get it over and done with. I wish I hadn't. This copper stood up and gave evidence claiming I'd said I had the can of deodorant because I was going to light it and burn someone with it. Lying bastard.

But for all his lies I was admonished and on my way home. I skived the train back to Edinburgh and was sitting having a pint and reflecting on a job well done in London when the phone went. It was the boys in the minibus asking where I was, because they'd hung around to take me home. I told them I was in Edinburgh enjoying a pint and they weren't best pleased, since they were still in London. But all was forgiven once they finally made it back up the road.

What we had achieved as a mob didn't really sink in for a few days. We'd gone to Millwall, smashed up their pub, battled with them twice and emerged virtually unscathed. Eventually, there would be a price to pay because Bobby, one of the boys charged with mobbing and rioting, was sentenced to three years in prison for his part in the battle. But it was a trip that gained the Capital City Service kudos from every other mob in Britain. Our reputation was sky high on the back of it. There was even a notice in the London *Evening Standard* that read: 'Congratulations Hibs on a job well done'. It was placed by West Ham's Inter City Firm.

Am I happy to say we went to The Den and lived to fight another day? You bet I am. Would I go back there?

Not on your bloody life.

17

THE AGONY AND THE ECSTASY

'Before Madness came on it all went tits up. I'll be honest, I was shitting bricks.'

Robert Morrice, 30, Edinburgh

While the 1990s had started with a bang, casuals were soon to grasp the full meaning of a boom-and-bust economy. For us, the highs of Millwall in 1990 and Anderlecht two years later would prove to be the exception rather than the rule.

There was a sign of things to come on 21 December 1992 when Madness played a gig at Ingliston. The CCS were going as a mob, not to cause trouble but because Madness were the business, they were a brilliant band and we'd all been fans right through the Eighties. The boys met up and had a few pints beforehand because this was a night when it wasn't about battling. The Nutty Boys were in town and our nutty boys were well up for seeing them. There were two other bands on the bill that night, The Farm and 808, but everyone was there for one band and one band only. Madness.

But as the boys arrived they spotted a few familiar faces

170

wandering around. At first they thought it was just the odd member of Rangers ICF who'd made the trip through, then a couple of Motherwell SS came strolling past. Glances were exchanged, none of them friendly, and it became clear this might well be a night when there could be madness offstage as well as on it. The glances soon became taunts and the atmosphere was getting uglier. Concertgoers who were just there for the music were getting nervous and who could blame them. If you've never been to Ingliston for a gig, it was just like a huge shed. The more affluent paid extra cash to have seats up on a small balcony but the ordinary punters were stood on a concrete floor and squeezed in. It was no place to have three angry mobs of casuals in the middle of the crowd.

The boys quickly assessed the situation and it wasn't looking good. This was no chance meeting as far as Rangers and Motherwell were concerned. The fact they were standing shoulder to shoulder meant they'd obviously arranged to come through and take us on, thinking we'd be caught by surprise. They'd managed to get the first part right. They'd met up. Surprise was not an option, and, now they'd been spotted, they had a decision to make. Did they take the lead and start the fight or wait and see what happened?

They chose to wait and see. Wrong option.

A cry of CCS went up and the boys waded in. Rangers and Motherwell met them halfway and a few assorted others decided they wanted a piece of the action. There were skinheads, stewards, you name it. Unfortunately for the CCS they were all on the same side and it wasn't ours. This was going to take a bit of sorting. As a mob we'd faced some tough situations before but we never imagined that the place we'd find ourselves most outnumbered was at Ingliston, at a gig. There was nothing else for it but to dig in because, at that moment, we knew Motherwell and Rangers were thinking this was a heaven-sent opportunity to make Hibs run on their own patch. They'd conveniently forgotten to mention they were double-handed as mobs and had a few freelance battlers chipping in as well. This, quite simply, was a fight the CCS could not afford to lose.

There was one piece of good fortune. The scaffolding poles left over from building the stage were on our side of the hall and they made handy weapons. It was a short, brutal battle in which a few Rangers and Motherwell heads got cracked and they were beaten back. Some skinhead who fancied his chances also collected a second prize and once all the screaming and shouting had subsided, and the stewards pretended they had restored order, the gig started.

You know the way it is at gigs where support acts get polite applause because nobody is really interested in them. Multiply that by ten for this concert and you get an idea of the atmosphere inside Ingliston. The regular concertgoers just wanted the support acts off, Madness on, and to get out of there as quickly as possible. It was a shame for them, it really was.

The mobs, meanwhile, just wanted the music to stop so they could start battling again because this one wasn't over, not by a long way. As each support act finished its set, a cry of CCS went up and the boys waded in again. There were no second thoughts when that cry went up. It was every man fighting not for himself, but for the name of the crew. That was where Rangers and Motherwell had a problem. They were away from home and they were an amalgamated mob. There was no sense of togetherness. They were just trying to pull a fly one.

Their back-up was ebbing away as well. After the first skirmish the skinheads were doing their best to blend into the background. The stewards had realised there were no easy pickings to be had either and that a shot at one of the CCS boys came at a heavy price. They were content to bide their time and let the mobs punch themselves out. In the end, they called the coppers, who at one stage were considering pulling the plug on the whole thing. They spoke to the promoters, who spoke to Madness and the band apparently said they'd play as long as their safety was guaranteed. Good old Madness. They were all football boys themselves, with Suggs being one of those celebrity Chelsea fans. But the coppers insisted the house lights had to stay up because they weren't prepared to run the risk of it all kicking-off again in a darkened hall.*

Madness played and they were brilliant. And, no, it didn't kick-off again. Rangers and Motherwell had learned their lesson. The CCS were still kings of their own territory. While that was a source of pride to us, it was also the biggest drawback. We were so dominant, particularly in and around Easter Road, that opposition mobs just stopped coming to face us. Aberdeen had gone through the same thing in the Eighties. They struggled to get mobs to come north and fight them because the result was almost a foregone conclusion. At their peak Aberdeen simply had too many bodies for any other mob to cope with. It was only when we smartened up our act and matched them tactically and with equal numbers that we were able to knock them off their perch.

But we were the first to admit it, travelling to Aberdeen back then was scary. You simply put that fear to one side and threw yourself into the fight. It appeared other mobs had lost the bottle to do that because we'd be hanging around Easter Road before games waiting for the opposition to arrive and there would be nothing. With that lack of action comes malaise and a few of the boys were getting disillusioned.

---

* The violence was so extreme, and the crushing so bad, that many people in the audience thought their lives were in danger. One fan told the *Daily Record* of his terrifying experience: 'I thought I was going to die. This young girl was being crushed, so I pulled her clear. Then I slipped and everybody piled on top of me. I remember thinking this was like Hillsborough.'

We'd still go on the road to try and get some action but the coppers had become pretty good at what they did as well. It was the Aberdeen coppers who had taken the lead and broken the back of their mob by doing some of them for mobbing and rioting. The old assault or breach-of-the-peace charges normally meant fines and any mob could live with that. Mobbing and rioting was a different kettle of fish. It normally meant jail time and boys weren't prepared to risk their jobs or, in some cases, their mortgages by getting banged up. To us this was still about having a bit of a roll around at the football. We genuinely didn't see ourselves as criminals, just people fighting other willing participants. But now the courts were sending our boys down for longer than people who'd robbed someone or broken into someone's house. They were the people we considered the real criminals.

But with the courts getting tougher, and the action getting scarcer, there was evidence people were drifting away from the CCS. The days of assembling a mob of two hundred for a battle were now a distant memory. The coppers were now using closed-circuit television to track us and it's almost impossible to get round that. It's no exaggeration to say that around that time we probably had a better idea than the coppers of which Edinburgh streets were covered by cameras. We had to. It meant the difference between getting nicked and getting away with it. The coppers were tilting the balance in their favour and they were taking no prisoners.

As I mentioned, we were still up for a battle on the road but the only place you were still likely to get one was Ibrox. By then, the Glasgow coppers had seen more than enough of us. They were sick of picking up bodies off Paisley Road West and we and the ICF tried arranging different meeting places to get it on. There was a leak somewhere because every time we had something arranged the coppers would be out in force at Queen Street. On four successive trips to Glasgow, the CCS stepped off the train and were immediately rounded up and chucked into police vans. We didn't even clap eyes on George Square on those four trips. We were just nabbed as soon as we got off the train, tossed into a van, taken up the road to the cop shop and banged up for the weekend. Then they ferried us down to Glasgow District Court on the Monday morning and we'd be fined £75 and sent on our way. I'm not arguing that we were angels or that we didn't have a fight set up. But I still thought you had to break the law before you could be arrested. Maybe I'm wrong, maybe there's a law that allowed them to arrest us for getting the train through to Glasgow.

Whatever the rights and wrongs of it, going on the road with the CCS was becoming an expensive pastime and it helped drive even more boys away. Unfortunately for us, as running with the CCS was becoming more expensive, kicks were proving considerably cheaper to find elsewhere. The club scene was blossoming and a lot of the boys were embracing it. It was a hell of a lot cheaper to buy an ecstasy tablet on a Friday night and rave the evening away than it was to get fined £75 in court on a Monday morning for travelling to a football match you didn't even get to see.

To begin with, the boys insisted they could combine both. But the effects of ecstasy and late nights saw more and more of them fail to show up on a Saturday for the football, because they just couldn't get out of their beds. The CCS was in danger of falling apart at that stage, because we were down to the hard core. We'd gone full circle and we were almost back where we started.

I've been asked the question many times: why didn't I join the ecstasy brigade and walk away as well? The answer is always the same. When I was a teenager I'd been one of the founder members of the CCS and it was a pride thing for me. Maybe I was guilty of not being able to let go but I was proud of what we'd achieved.

We'd built ourselves up from Uncle Dougie's Soccer Hooligans to the most-feared mob in Scotland. I wasn't about to let all that go for the sake of popping a pill on a Friday night.

Drugs weren't for me anyway. Around the time the CCS was formed Edinburgh had become smack city. It was the heroin capital of Britain and, believe me, I'd had more than one chance to go down the drugs route. I'd shunned it then and I shunned it again in the Nineties. I'd seen kids I'd been at school with become shells of human beings thanks to drugs. Christ, guys I'd been at school with were six-feet-under thanks to drugs. I preferred a fight I could win. More than that, I was still a Hibs fan. When push came to shove, even if the mob was running out of steam, I still wanted to watch Hibs on a Saturday. It didn't matter if they were good, bad or downright lousy, they were still my team and getting fucked up on a Friday night and missing the game was a non-starter, fight or no fight.

It wasn't all doom and gloom, however. We did manage to out-fox the cops in 1994 after getting a call from Rangers. They were due to play at Easter Road but didn't want to take the chance of arranging a battle anywhere near the ground in case the coppers got wind of it and just nicked the lot of us. We suggested that instead of getting the train from Queen Street they travelled from Central station instead. There was a train from there that was a real pain in the arse because it stopped everywhere in darkest Lanarkshire. The train from Queen Street took forty-five minutes; this bloody thing took an hour-and-a-half because it stopped in places like Shotts and Livingston. It was no tour of Scotland's high spots but it was a train the coppers were unlikely to be watching. It also made a stop in Edinburgh at a place called Slateford, which is just up the road from Hearts' Tynecastle ground. It was deep in enemy territory for us but, hey, beggars couldn't be choosers and fights were few and far between by then. Rangers were game for it and they agreed to get off the train at Slateford, where we would be waiting for them. We put the word round that there was a battle on the go and the response was predictable. The hard core were in and a lot of boys we hadn't seen for weeks indicated they were up for it as well. Some even agreed to forego their Friday-night ecstasy for the occasion.

In the end, the battle probably did the CCS more harm than good. It was a disaster, a total bloody disaster. With the Glasgow coppers being so active we hadn't had a decent scrap with Rangers for ages and, as a result, we had no idea their crew had dwindled as much as ours. The difference was we could get still get boys out for the big occasions. We had a hundred boys waiting at Slateford station. There were forty Rangers on the train and some of them were petrified rookies. When the train pulled into Slateford, some of these boys took one look at the size of our mob and refused point blank to get off the train. Their top boy was having none of that. They were ordered to get off and join the mob and it was a complete mismatch.

Fair play to Rangers, they gave it a go when a lot of mobs would just have cowered on the train as they realised they were completely outnumbered. They came charging down the platform but it was a mismatch, a total mismatch. The fight spilled out of the station and on to the road outside but Rangers got an absolute doing, in hind-sight too much of a doing. A few of them wound up in hospital, most probably the ones who shouldn't have been there in the first place.

I don't know what the Rangers boys were thinking about. It was a suicide mission and one they could have avoided like every crew was doing when they came to Edinburgh. Being game was one thing. Being stupid was quite another. That was a lesson we'd learned ten years earlier. It seemed the lesson still hadn't got through to Rangers. Any excitement or buzz the boys got from that battle didn't last long. If anything, it had merely confirmed what a lot of them were thinking. The glory days looked like they were over. If Rangers could only muster a ragtag band of forty, half of them useless, for a pre-arranged battle in Edinburgh, then casual mobs were in terminal decline.

* * *

At least there still foreign climes to look forward to because the mobs abroad were still going as strong as ever. Scotland had arranged a Friday-night friendly against Holland in Utrecht to be played on 27 May 1994. The phone lines had been busy before the match and a battle was pre-arranged between the CCS and some of the Aberdeen mob on one side, and a load of Dutch on the other. The boys got into the country undetected, no mean feat in itself given our past history in Holland.

They made it to the main square in Utrecht without alerting the coppers and the battle kicked off. It was a good one too although I don't think the good burghers of Utrecht would have agreed. They were going about their normal Friday-afternoon business when our joint mob came roaring across the square to take on the Dutch. There were bars with tables and chairs outside but they were soon flying through the air as battle was joined. The Dutch were also tooled up for the occasion and you needed to have your wits about you just to avoid getting stabbed or slashed as the fighting became hand to hand and boot to boot.

But, as was the way in the Nineties, the coppers had obviously been biding their time. It took less than a couple of minutes for them to swoop in big numbers. There was no escape, they had the area surrounded. A total of forty-six Scottish boys were lifted and the newspapers had another field day. The CCS got the blame with Aberdeen getting a passing mention. Most of the boys escaped with fines and were kicked out of the country but that's the one good thing about the Dutch. They don't hold a grudge. They'll kick you out but they'll also let you back in next time you want to go. I'd imagine it drove the authorities in this country crazy that they weren't tougher on us. But that's the Dutch all over. Laid back, devil may care, they were so used to dealing with violence when Ajax and Feyenoord met that their coppers just saw it as another day at the office. They weren't even unpleasant when they nicked you. I suppose from their point of view we were small time, because when Ajax and Feyenoord got it on it wasn't unknown for fans to be killed.

International football was definitely the way ahead for us. The domestic scene had become so stagnant and the coppers so proficient at being one step ahead that wreaking havoc in other countries seemed the only option. The coppers were even assigning spotters to us by that stage. We'd experienced it on European trips but now we had plain-clothes guys with us everywhere. Even if you went to the toilet in a railway station, you were checking out the other blokes trying to work out which one was the CID guy.

But just when it seemed as though our race was run, Scotland only went and qualified for Euro 96. And, guess what, the tournament was being staged in England. Even better, Scotland were drawn in the same group as the hosts. A Saturday-afternoon match at Wembley. It would be just like the good old days.

We decided to keep our powder dry because the cops were all over this tournament like a rash. Keeping a low profile in the run-up to the England game was a priority or we'd be rumbled before we'd even seen any action. We decided to drive down south in a fleet of cars, about sixty of us all told. We based ourselves in High Barnet, near Scotland's training base, and everything went to plan. We arrived the night before the game, fixed ourselves up with accommodation, and made a few calls to confirm our battle plan. We'd already arranged a pre-meet with some of our former pals from Oldham and they agreed to come to High Barnet for a battle on the morning of the game.

There was a pub just down the road from our digs with a good-sized car park outside it and that was to be the battleground. On the Saturday morning we wandered along to the boozer for opening time and sank a couple of pints as we waited for our rivals to appear. Bang on time, 11:30, their minibus came around the corner. We formed our battle lines, expecting the minibus doors to fly open and them to launch themselves at us. The minibus doors didn't open. In fact, the minibus didn't even stop. The boys inside just looked out of the windows at us as they sped off in the direction of London. Maybe they'd seen the size of our mob and bottled it, I'll never know for certain. At least they had the decency to look embarrassed as they drove past and there could only have been a dozen of them. Even the English mobs were struggling to raise numbers. They'd done what Rangers should have done at Slateford and let discretion be the better part of valour. But it was like a kick in the nuts for us. All that way and nothing to show for it.

And now our own mob was split. Half of the boys wanted to head into London and take on the English after the game. Me? I just felt so deflated by the whole thing I simply couldn't be bothered. I just wanted to get away and the guys who had travelled in our car felt exactly the same way. There were no arguments and no hard feelings; at least I don't think there were.

It was just accepted that at that moment our mob was going to head in two different directions. A load of the boys made for London and they got what they wanted later that night. They had the mother and father of all battles with the English in Trafalgar Square and restored some Scottish pride after the team's 2–0 defeat.

The rest of us jumped into cars and headed north. We stopped off at a pub to watch the game, then drove on to Blackpool. We spent the weekend there before heading back to Edinburgh. Another weekend had been wasted.

* * *

Things were going from bad to worse back home. We couldn't have organised a fight if we'd offered to send a guy along on his own to take on an opposition mob. They'd have thought it was a trap. So it was ironic that one of our biggest battles of the late Nineties came about purely by chance.

It was derby day against Hearts and we were doing our usual – walking to Tynecastle. Because things had quietened down so much we hadn't even bothered taking the traditional route towards Haymarket and up Gorgie Road. We'd decided to cut down through Tollcross and get to Gorgie that way. As we were walking past the Polwarth Tavern one of the boys said, very quietly, 'Bingo.' We stopped and looked to see what he was pointing at and there they were. The Hearts mob, in all their glory, sitting laughing and joking, as if they hadn't a care in the world.

Well, they did now.

I don't know what they must have thought as the doors of the pub were battered open and we came steaming in. God, it felt good. After all the frustrations of recent years we were back doing what we did best. Normally, Hearts would have scarpered but this time they had no choice. There was no way out the door for them, we had it sealed off. They had to stand and fight but they knew the game was up. The pub got trashed, they got a hiding and we were off our marks again, splitting up so that the coppers didn't have a big gang to pounce on when they started looking for us. Twos and threes were the order of the day because we knew we were safe from attack. The Hearts mob would still be patching themselves up back at the Polwarth. The Joe Breezy swagger was in our step that day as we ambled the rest of the way to Tynecastle.

The boys were back in town.

18

HITLER'S MISSUS

There are times when you just know it's going to be a bad day and 9 April 2000 was one of those times. Hibs were playing Aberdeen in a Scottish Cup semi-final at Hampden Park. Not put too fine a point on it, the Hibees were playing crap at the time. They'd got to the semis thanks to a series of decent draws but none of us were kidding ourselves this was going to be a glory day and an end to the long wait for the Scottish Cup triumph we all craved.

Not even the fact that it was Aberdeen we were facing could raise spirits. The glory days of two-hundred-a-side battles were long gone. The split of the 1990s had weakened our mob and Aberdeen really weren't that much better off than us. That was why I broke with tradition that day and had a right skinful before I went to the ground. In days gone by that would have been a no-no but not today. With no decent prospect of a fight there was no reason to keep my wits about me.

We'd decided that win, lose or draw we'd make a day of it so we headed through to Glasgow early. This was a rare luxury, the chance to enjoy an outing at the football without having to keep a clear head for the battle ahead. There were no last-minute plans to be gone through, there were no nerves. Nothing. Just getting bevvied enough to be in a good mood; but not so bevvied that the coppers would knock us back at the turnstiles.

It was a right good day. We'd settled into a pub in the centre of town but old habits die hard. We couldn't stop ourselves keeping one eye on the door, just in case marauding Aberdeen boys took us by surprise or we were caught on the hop by Rangers. After all, we were right in the heart of their city. As it turned out, neither of those things happened and, after a good few pints, we headed round to Central station to catch the train to Mount Florida. This was another first for us; public transport to the ground. When we got off at Mount Florida we still had time to kill so I went into the local newsagent's shop and bought a packet of fags.

We were standing at the corner we'd turn to take us down to the Rangers end at Hampden Park and I was wrestling with the cellophane wrapper on this packet of cigarettes. Never mind a lager head, I had lager fingers. I'd have had more chance of opening the fags wearing boxing gloves. One of my mates was watching me wrestling unsuccessfully with the box and he said, 'Jesus, Dykes. Give them here. No chance of smoking being fatal for you. You can't even open the pack.' He opened the packet with practised fingers and planted a cigarette right between my lips.

But no sooner had he done that than a van pulled up and out jumped a bunch of the ASC. Bevvied or not, we were in battle mode, albeit a little more slowly than normal. I was still standing there with the unlit fag hanging from my mouth as they piled towards us. And, as I prepared to wade in, a voice shouted 'Dykes'. I spun around and there was an Edinburgh CID spotter.

The CID had obviously sent through some of their men to keep an eye out for any trouble and their eyes would have lit up when they saw there were only twelve CCS boys there. But they had enough experience to appreciate that even twelve of us could cause a battle if the opportunity arose. The problem was that now he'd clocked me and called me by name I couldn't raise a finger to help the lads. As soon as I made a move he'd have me nicked because he'd made it clear he knew who I was. He'd already made a positive identification without the use of the closed-circuit television.

There was nothing I could do but, as it turned out, I didn't need to do anything. The coppers were on the scene before anything more than some serious posturing took place and they quickly split up the rival factions. I shot the Edinburgh CID guy a look as we were ushered towards the ground. That was all I needed, coppers tailing me wherever I went.

I don't know if it was that, or the lager, or the fact we'd been caught completely cold by Aberdeen. But, whatever the reason, I was in a lousy mood by the time we completed the short walk to Hampden. I'd hazard a guess it was a combination of all three but it would be just that, a guess. In any case, I was no ray of sunshine as we shuffled up to the turnstiles.

It was the usual farce for a Scottish Cup semi at Hampden that didn't involve the Old Firm. You'd be lucky if there were going to be 25,000 fans there so the ground would be half empty, yet the game was all-ticket. It's not as if it makes it any quicker at the turnstiles, either. It still takes an eternity and I was getting more and more pissed-off by the second.

Once we'd finally got into the ground we headed off to get something to eat before taking our seats. It turned out my ticket was for the row in front of my mates but I just grabbed a spare seat beside them. Our little area wasn't going to be full and there were plenty of empty seats around us. But there's something unique about the stewards at Hampden. They are employed by the same company that provides stewards for a load of other grounds in

Scotland but the Hampden ones are special. They have an attitude all their own. And this was my day to encounter a right little Hitler, a female Hitler at that. I was sitting talking to my mates when I got a tap on the shoulder and looked up to see a rotund woman with her eyes narrowed as she stared at me.

'You're in the wrong seat,' she bellowed. She didn't say it pleasantly; she didn't keep her voice down. She bellowed it. 'Look,' I said, 'there are plenty of empty seats all around this area. I'm just sitting next to my mates.'

'It doesn't matter,' she said. 'This guy's ticket is for this seat and you are in the wrong seat.' As she bellowed the word 'you', she pointed at me like some demented traffic cop. I looked at the guy whose seat I was in and said, 'Look, my seat is in the row in front, just there,' and I pointed to it. He seemed happy enough to move but Hitler's missus was having none of it.

'No,' she said, 'you move. Shift your arse now.' I'd had enough of her by then and the black cloud was descending again. 'Look,' I said, 'why don't you just fuck off.' My mates dissolved into fits of laughter and the guy moved into my seat, happy enough to be out of the firing line. And that was that, or so I thought.

Instead, Hitler's missus had gone to get the coppers and she returned with two of them, pointing at me and bellowing about being verbally abused and how she wasn't paid to be spoken to like that. To be fair to the coppers, they tried to reason with me but by this point I was in a shouting match with Hitler's missus. Their words weren't getting through to me because the black cloud had become red mist and all logic had gone. The cops grabbed me by either arm and I was battling with them, trying to free up an arm to take a swing.

That's why getting boozed-up before a game was always a no-no for me. You lose all self-control and, when you have battles to fight, you need to know when the other guy has had enough or you wind up killing someone. But that day I was out of control. The coppers had to drag me kicking and screaming and cursing all the way round to the back of the Rangers end where the ground's holding cells are. They handed me over to another couple of coppers and I tried to battle with them as well.

I have to admit those were not my proudest moments. Battling with the coppers was just madness, the sort of thing that could turn a simple fine for breach of the peace into a jail sentence for assaulting a police officer. It didn't take me long to calm down once I was chucked into the holding cell, although my mood didn't improve when I heard the Aberdeen fans singing joyfully as their team went in front.

By the time the van came to ferry the wrongdoers to their various cells for the night, I was totally depressed. For one thing, the parched mouth that is a by-product of a morning on the lager was now a factor. I had the beginnings of a headache as well and I knew that I was looking at a weekend locked up before court on the Monday morning. Oh, and Hibs, as expected, had lost.

When I got to court on the Monday morning I'd had the same result, a sickener. Resisting arrest had been added to the breach of the peace on my charge sheet and, given my previous record, a quick fine and slap on the wrist was a non-starter. I was bailed to appear at a later date.

By the time I got home I was gutted. Another lost weekend and the prospect of a whopping fine or worse to come. I was in a deep depression for a couple of months, which was only made worse by the negative publicity after the CCS battle with the Tartan Army on the way to a Scotland game in Arnhem (see chapter 19). I'd decided I'd had enough of all this stuff at the football. I had to make a clean break. A job advert in a newspaper caught my eye; it was for a steel mill in Eindhoven in Holland. I gave the number a call and it turned out they were looking for people to start right away. I had no ties, nothing to keep me in Scotland, so that was it. Count me in. I hooked up with the boys later on that night and told them I would be giving the CCS a miss for a while because I was going away to work.

Now, I know what you're thinking. What about the court appearance? I didn't give it a second thought and neither did any of the boys when I told them I was off to Holland to work. Maybe that tells you something about life as a football casual. I'd been grabbed by the cops umpteen times for unpaid fines but that wasn't because you deliberately set out not to pay them, although to let the odd one or two slide would have been a help financially. It was simply because you had a whole series of fines on the go at the one time. It was one of the drawbacks of fighting at football most weeks. So another court appearance, with another fine to come, was normal to me and I simply put it out of my mind until the letter confirming a court date arrived.

My parents couldn't understand it any better than any other ordinary person. My mother would always say: 'Anything that happens to you is your own doing,' and she was right. My dad always insisted he could make more sense of all the fighting and travelling if I was getting paid to do it. I think he'd have been happier if I had been a professional boxer.

But I went off to Holland and wound-up spending fifteen months there although I did come home on a few occasions, most notably for a memorable trip to London with some of my CCS mates (see chapter 20). It was a nice change of pace, and the first time I'd ever worked away from home. All my working life had been spent alongside my dad. He was a self-employed building contractor and his business had always done pretty well. I'd started working with him as a teenage apprentice and worked my way up to become a time-served painter and decorator. It wasn't all wine and roses. He'd sacked me more than once when a weekend with the CCS had meant I was still in the cells on a Monday morning when I should have been reporting for work. But he always took me back because he wouldn't see me stuck and, although I say it myself, I was a good worker when I was there.

Holland, therefore, would be a complete change for me and I thoroughly enjoyed it. I went to watch PSV Eindhoven play from time to time while keeping an eye on events surrounding Hibs from afar. I even caught a flight to Athens to watch Hibs play AEK. I was pretty flush at the time because I was earning good money so I treated myself and flew business class. Very nice it was too. Waited on hand and foot, this was the life.

As soon as the plane touched down in Athens I headed into the centre of town, figuring I'd catch up with a few familiar faces. I hadn't bothered phoning them because it had been a spur-of-the-moment thing. Anyway, it would be worth it to see their faces when I came strolling down the street. In the end, it was me who got the surprise. I bumped into a couple of Hibs scarfers and asked them where the rest of the support was. They told me there was hardly anyone there, what with the game being postponed. Postponed? Since when? They looked at me as if I had three heads. Since 9/11 happened. The attack on the Twin Towers had forced the postponement of the match. I'd had a wasted journey. But the boys were good enough to let me crash on their hotel floor for the night and I had a very nice flight back to Holland the next day.

At that time being a bail jumper was the furthest thing from my mind, until I finally came home. As soon as I became aware of what I'd done, there was only one thing for it. I went straight down to the local police station, explained what had happened and turned myself in. Maybe naively, I expected a sympathetic hearing when I went to court. Let's face it: what I had done was clean up my act. I'd gone and found gainful employment, albeit in breach of my bail conditions, I was planning to make a fresh start now I was home and the CCS days were a distant memory.

I'm afraid the pleas for clemency fell on deaf ears. I was sentenced to four months in prison and that was me, off to the dreaded Bar-L again. As I've told you before, that's a place you pray you never see the inside of once, never mind twice. But at least second time around I was older and a lot more streetwise and I wasn't shiting myself the way I had been when I was eighteen.

I suppose, having been inside that jail once, the fear of the unknown was gone. It still didn't make it a pleasant experience. Barlinnie prison is just horrible. As soon as I was back inside the clanging of doors and the shouts of the other inmates were all too familiar. And unlike the first time I'd been inside, I had no choice this time but to wear prison-issue clothes. They're awful. They stink and they're never properly clean. In fact, the whole place stinks. In the mornings the jail stinks of, well, you can imagine, with all those guys slopping out their chamber pots. The rest of the day it reeks of detergent and bleach. But I just kept my head down, kept out of trouble and resolved to continue the policy of turning over a new leaf once I was released. This time I was certain I was finished with the CCS.

How wrong can you be?

19

STEAMING INTO THE TARTAN ARMY

The town of Arnhem became famous during the Second World War because there was a bridge there that the Allies were desperate to secure, but couldn't. Unfortunately, we managed to get into a war before we even reached Arnhem.

The local football team, Vitesse Arnhem, had spent millions building a new stadium called the Gelredome. It had everything, including a pitch that was moved outside on giant rollers so it got plenty of sunlight. The new stadium was to be officially opened with an international friendly between Holland and Scotland on 26 April 2000. Now that was an occasion not to be missed. There was bound to be action because Dutch fans are tasty, with both Ajax and Feyenoord regularly battling on the domestic front.

Around fifty of the CCS decided to make the trip. Rather than make the long trek to the south coast we discovered there was a ferry crossing from Newcastle to Nijmegen. That was ideal. We'd get the train to Newcastle, catch the overnight ferry to Nijmegen, hop on a train at Nijmegen and head to Amsterdam. From there, we could get the train to Arnhem on the day of the game. Perfect.

The mob of us met up the day we were leaving, had a couple of beers on the train down to Newcastle and boarded the ship. And everything was fine, it really couldn't have been better. We were on the ferry, minding our own business and having a great laugh. There was a load of Scotland fans on the ferry as well and they seemed to be in good spirits, although we gave them a wide berth. We didn't take much to do with the Tartan Army.

As it got late the boys drifted off one by one to grab a bit of shut-eye. By around one, maybe two in the morning, there were just four of us left sitting at a table in the bar area outside the ship's disco. Just in front of us there were a couple of girls sitting at another table having a quiet drink. Well, it would have been a quiet drink if this idiot in a kilt hadn't been giving them his best chat-up lines. Honest to God, they would have made your toes curl. But he was one of those sad cases you come across with the Tartan Army, dressed in his Scotland top and kilt, and who thinks he's the funniest guy alive. And he was trying, and failing miserably, to chat up this girl. Everyone but him could see she wasn't in the slightest bit interested. The look on her face suggested she'd have locked herself in a convent rather than let him anywhere near her. But this boy just wasn't picking up the signals because he was bevvied. He was becoming a bit of a pest and he was basically harassing her. We were thinking of having a word with him but fortunately he gave up the ghost and went away.

Once he'd shambled off my wee cousin went over and started talking to the two girls and their mood changed completely. They were finally being engaged in conversation by a sober, well-dressed Scotsman. Within a couple of minutes the two girls had come over to our table and joined us and they admitted they were glad to be shot of the drunk. So everything was fine and my cousin was getting on famously with the girl who had been harassed by the drunk.

Sadly, our nice wee night was interrupted as the idiot in the kilt reappeared. He headed straight for our table and shouted at my cousin, 'That's my bird you're talking to.' The girls insisted they hadn't clapped eyes on this guy before they boarded the ferry. So I said to him, 'Look mate, we're going to Amsterdam. You can have any bird you want there for £30. So we're not going to have an argument over a bird now, are we?'

But this guy was having none of it.

'That's my bird ya bastard.'

Then he went over to where my cousin was sitting, stood right in front of him, and just lifted his kilt right up. He had nothing on underneath the kilt so everything was hanging out there for the world to see. His bits were right in front of my wee cousin's face, practically touching his skin. And this numbskull had a stupid grin on his ugly, fat, sweaty face, as if he thought this was the funniest thing he'd ever done. The Tartan Army, eh? Pure class.

Now the only reason this idiot was grinning was because he couldn't see what was coming. But I could. I knew what I would have done in the same situation. I'd have decked him there and then. I was amazed my cousin still hadn't moved a muscle. Instead he gave him the chance to back off, then politely asked him to move and got 'That's my bird' as a reply. And then he got up and nutted him, and he moved so quickly Mr Kilt didn't see it coming. He dropped like a stone and was spark out before he hit the deck.

Now, as I said, we were sitting outside the ship's disco and that area was sectioned off with two-way glass. The folk inside the disco could see us but we couldn't see them. So what we didn't know was that Mr Kilt wasn't a solo drunk. He had about thirty of his mates with him, and they'd seen the whole thing unfold from inside the disco. The next thing we know, they're coming screaming towards the door, pointing fingers, calling my cousin for everything and threatening all sorts.

That was it. Nice night over; let battle commence. We launched ourselves towards the door because we knew if the thirty of them got through it, we'd had it. It's an old trick that one: keep the first wave penned in the doorway and nobody else can get out. So there we were getting steamed into these Tartan Army arseholes when the ship's crew appeared out of nowhere, carrying wooden truncheons. Presumably the call had gone out that there was a riot on board because it wasn't just one or two crewmen who appeared – there was a whole squad of them.

Suddenly, we were piggy in the middle. The Tartan Army were swinging at us from the front; the crew were knocking seven shades of shit out of us from behind with their wooden truncheons. I don't care where you're from or what you've done: that's not fair, especially when it was the phantom flasher who started the whole thing. You can only take so many whacks with those truncheons before the fight goes out of you and the crew quickly regained control.

It might have been nice if the two girls had spoken up in our defence but not a bit of it. They'd got off their mark as soon as it kicked off. In the aftermath of the fight the CCS boy who lived in Motherwell had a bad head wound and after he got stitched up he was thrown in the brig; the rest of us were ordered to hand over our passports. They told us to report to the purser's office in the morning to reclaim them. So we figured that was it. Another day, another battle, but we'd be fine. All we had to do was pick up our passports in the morning, avoid an angry mob of Tartan Army foot soldiers, and get on our way. We found a quiet spot on the ship, away from the angry mob, and grabbed a couple of hours' sleep.

By the time we woke up, we had almost reached port. We made a beeline for the purser's office to get our passports back because we just wanted to get off the ship before we got into another battle with Mr Kilt's mates. The purser told us to wait a couple of minutes but by this time the ship was docking so we asked what was going on. There were four chairs opposite his office and the purser told us to sit there and wait.

At times like that you get a bad feeling and this bad feeling was fully justified. Before anybody was allowed to disembark, there was the clunk of heavy, booted feet coming up the gangway. The riot squad came aboard. Your first thought is, 'Oh no.' They clunked over to the purser's office and they were handed our passports. They checked the photograph on each one and looked across at us, matching the names to the faces.

At that point I was certain we were getting lifted. I wondered if they would settle for keeping us on the ship and sending us straight back to Newcastle, which wouldn't have been the worst option. I don't think the crew fancied that option so that was us, hauled off by the riot squad. We were dragged off the ship first, in front of all the other passengers, which wasn't the best. In fact, it was downright embarrassing.

The coppers loaded us into a van and we were taken to the police station in the port. They asked us to give a statement and we all gave the same one. We all said we had been attacked. The police, unfortunately, wouldn't swallow a word of it. They insisted witnesses on the ship had told the crew that a fellow in a kilt was the victim of an unprovoked assault in the form of a head butt. Unbelievable. Still, we consoled ourselves with the notion that Mr Kilt would wind up getting his comeuppance in Amsterdam. He'd pay for a prostitute, then argue with anyone else who wanted her services. What an arsehole.

But he was free and we weren't. We were ushered into another van and taken on a drive through the Dutch countryside. We must have driven for half an hour, forty minutes maybe. We asked the driver where he was going but he wasn't telling us anything. The van eventually reached some sort of compound and it drove into an underground area. People arrived to unload us and get our bags out of the van and we were handed them and directed towards a lift, with our escort following us.

The lift took us all the way up to what we later found out was the top floor of this place. Once we got out, there was some kind of reception desk straight ahead of us. We got checked in at the desk, but were still allowed to keep our bags and our money. I'd never come across this before. Then we were told we were being moved along to cells. We walked down a long, brightly-lit corridor, and I could see all these cells with hatches on them. I thought we were in some kind of upmarket police station. Then we reached the end of the corridor and the guy escorting us told us to leave our bags there.

I knew it had been too good to be true. I was getting ready for the order to hand over our money and our fags. But, no, they let us keep our cash and cigarettes. I resolved to write a letter to the Scottish coppers, telling them they should consult their Dutch counterparts on how to treat people in the cells, if this was going to be the order of the day. Then we were shown through another door and into a room with couches and televisions and big windows. That's when I twigged where they'd brought us. We were at Schiphol airport. Because we were on the top floor of the building there was a panoramic view and that's where we were – at the airport. This wasn't a cop shop, it was the immigration centre. We were being detained as illegal foreign nationals. Well, that was certainly a new one on me. I'd been detained as many things but never as an illegal alien.

Anyway, in this place there was a lounge, then you went through a door and there was a shower area. Going through another door took you to the sleeping quarters, which were bunk beds. I know it's selfish but I was so glad I had three mates in there with me because conversation would have been at a premium otherwise. Unsurprisingly, there weren't many English-speaking detainees. One guy was from Macedonia and he sat jabbering away to us. Macedonia was the only word we could understand.

Late on the first night, I was lying in my bunk when a big African bloke was brought in. I asked what time it was and he just ignored me. 'Fine,' I thought and went back to sleep. But on the second morning the four of us were up and about and the only channel we could watch on the telly was British Eurosport. That was the only channel we would understand.

The African bloke wasn't the ignorant so-and-so I'd first figured him for. It turned out he hadn't understood a word I'd said that first night. He obviously liked his sport because although he couldn't speak any English he sat and watched Eurosport with us. We all got on fine with him and we told him that he should claim asylum. At first he didn't understand what we meant but we eventually got the message across and he was off shouting asylum at anyone who would listen. I always wondered if he got it in the end.

The lousy food and the temperature aside, it really wasn't the worst place in which to be banged up. Put it this way, it was no Barlinnie. But the big windows meant that when the temperature soared outside, it soared inside. One day the temperature in the centre hit thirty degrees centigrade and the room at the top of the building was scorching. We were melting and, obviously, the windows didn't open. Or we'd have been offski. But those were the only complaints. The rest of it was fine. We were even allowed to go and get shower gel and soap and stuff and a change of clothes from our bags.

We could also phone home so it was a bit like being in a hotel. The only thing you couldn't do was leave and all four us were getting seriously bored at being cooped-up. All we really wanted to know was what was happening, how long we were going to be kept there, but nobody could tell us. As the boredom really kicked in, all we wanted to do was go home. Because we had money we even asked some of the staff in the centre to nip into Amsterdam and buy us some porn, anything to keep us occupied, but they wouldn't do it.

But there were some poor-looking souls in that place. When you went to use the phone you could see into some of the cells. The ones near the phone housed the drug mules, the people who had swallowed packages of drugs to try and avoid detection at airports. All these cells contained people who'd been caught doing that and they were in a right state. They weren't allowed out of their cells until the drugs had passed through them, if you catch my drift.

But, finally, on our fourth day in the centre, we got some news. A bloke came in and told us there had been such a long delay because the authorities had hoped the ferry company would agree to take us back. They'd accepted the original crew didn't want anything to do with us but they'd hoped another crew would agree to have us on board. Apparently, all the crew members from that company stuck together and said there was no way it was going to happen so we'd be stuck there until the Dutch authorities could arrange a flight. We thought we'd got a real result with that because it was only a short hop from Amsterdam to Edinburgh on a plane and he'd told us we were getting flown home. That put a wee spring in our step as we packed up our stuff and got taken back down in the lift.

Once we reached our floor we were dumped in a big holding cell with a load of folk we hadn't seen before from other parts of the immigration centre. These were obviously the people who were being kicked out of the country. There was a woman sitting rocking backwards and forwards in a chair and wailing. The next minute she went berserk and started hammering her head against the wall. The four of us jumped about a foot in the air when she started that carry-on. What a fright she gave us. But the guards were in quickly to jump on her, and she was obviously a nutter.

Then we got transferred to a cell, just the four of us. Six policemen came in and laid down the law, as policemen do. They told us they were our escort but they weren't going to put handcuffs on us for the flight to Newcastle. Newcastle? What happened to Edinburgh? Apparently, the way deportation works is that you're sent back to your point of departure and ours was Newcastle. We didn't want to complain in case they sent us back up to the sixth floor to watch more British Eurosport. But at least they weren't going to cuff us. Instead they would be sitting all around us so that if we misbehaved they'd be on us in a flash. I was looking forward to having a beer on the plane but that was another no-no. No drink allowed. Just as well it was a short flight.

We got taken on to the plane first and they sat us right up the very back, away from all the other passengers. We didn't misbehave on the flight; we were just delighted to be getting home. But even then it wasn't that simple. We figured it would be a case of getting off the plane in Newcastle, picking up our bags, and Bob's your uncle. Not a bit of it. Unlike on the ship, everyone else was allowed to disembark before us. We were the last ones off, surrounded by our escort and there was a big van full of police waiting to meet us.

It was overkill. There were three times as many cops as there were of us. The official handover was done at the airport police station in Newcastle. We were signed for and we became the property of the Geordie police. Then they wanted to interview us all over again. We were asked all the same questions we'd been asked in Nijmegen, and we gave exactly the same statements.

I admit I was thinking we were going to get done, because there was too much fuss being made simply to let us go. There was also the fact that there was a media scrum outside the airport police station.

Sky Television had a camera crew there and there was the usual band of newspaper reporters and photographers. But the police even screwed up the media by smuggling us out the back door of the station – in a mail van, of all things. They drove us out of the airport and dropped us at this metro station in the middle of nowhere. They told us the metro would take us into the centre of Newcastle. We caught the metro, headed into Newcastle and didn't even bother hanging around. We went straight to the train station and caught the first train back to Edinburgh.

We were knackered, we were pissed off and we just wanted to get home. As the train reached Edinburgh the sign for Waverley station was a welcome sight. But as we got off the train, and made our way across the station concourse, there was a flash. Then another, and then a third. Bloody photographers from the *Daily Record*. And before long there's a reporter running breathlessly alongside you, asking the usual inane questions. 'Are you ashamed of what you did?' 'How do you feel about dragging the Tartan Army's good name through the mud?' No, and go ask Mr Kilt how he feels about dragging the Tartan Army's good name through the mud. More notoriety. Just what we needed.

There's never a mail van around when you need one, is there?*

---

* Predictably, the media and the football establishment blamed the CCS for the trouble on the ferry. The *Daily Record* reported how 'real' Scots fans 'condemned the thugs' for shaming Scotland. While SFA security advisor William McDougall said of the CCS, 'They were obviously intent on causing trouble . . . our reputation is spoiled by the likes of this.' To be fair, the *Record* did at least give the CCS the chance to put its side of the story and quoted Derek Dykes as saying: 'They [the Tartan Army] just attacked us with everything they could lay their hands on. We were fighting at least thirty people with kilts on. Then security guards attacked us too. It must be easier to attack three people rather than thirty drunk Scotland fans.'

20

SKY'S THE LIMIT

If you fancied a change of scenery what would you do? Rent a cottage in the country perhaps? Go for a drive? Take in a movie? For us, in the year 2000, fights were almost becoming a thing of the past. Foreign trips still brought their fair share of rucks but not every away game could guarantee what we were looking for. For example, on 2 September 2000 Scotland were playing in Latvia, of all places. The fixtures had been arranged a year in advance and we'd scouted all the potential hot spots. There weren't any. Latvia certainly wasn't one of them so we weren't going there.

I was home from Eindhoven for a week's holiday and one of the boys had written to the Saturday-morning Sky Sports-show *Soccer AM* to see if we could get on it. They had a bunch of fans from a different club on every week and we fancied representing Hibs. Naturally, the club's directors would have had a fit if they had learned we were planning to be the face of Hibs on a popular television programme but fortunately they were none the wiser. The only stipulation in our letter to the programme makers was that we could only come to the studios on an international weekend. We weren't about to miss a Hibs game to ponce around in London.

So there we were, wondering how we'd fill a blank weekend on the football calendar, when a letter dropped through one of the boys' doors. It was from Sky, asking us if we could fill the fan zone on *Soccer AM* on 2 September. Now that was what you called perfect. No Hibs game to miss, Scotland off for a kick in the Baltics, and us off to London. What were we going to do for a change of scenery? We were going on the telly. There were seven of us planning to make the trip and the rest of the boys were green with envy. This was a show most of us watched on a Saturday before we met up in Edinburgh; it was a favourite with fans of most teams. And now the CCS boys were going to be on it. It didn't get any better than this.

The plan was to go down to London on the Friday afternoon, get settled into our hotel for the night and have a few beers. With only seven of us on the trip, we didn't bother phoning any mobs down south. Avoiding them would be the order of the day on this outing. Running into them – especially some of the mobs with long memories, like Millwall – might prove to be our last-ever action. We caught the Friday-morning train from Edinburgh and were in London by the middle of the afternoon. After a few beers near King's Cross station, we jumped into a couple of cabs and headed out to the hotel, which was handy for the studios. We had our instructions for the following morning: Sky would send a minibus to collect us at six; the show didn't start until ten, but they wanted us there early.

That, you would have thought, would have meant we took it easy the night before. Not a bit of it. The CCS was on tour again, for the first time in years. That night it was great crack. The seven of us sat there and swapped stories about the good old days. A charge often levelled against casual groups is that they're too fond of reliving past glories. Journalists use that one all the time. I'd always argue that when you have the sort of memories and common bond we had as a group, those past experiences are something to cherish. The camaraderie of those days never leaves you, no matter how great your life after the CCS is.

So we downed beer after beer, with precious little food mixed in, as we strolled down memory lane. The only problem was that when we looked at the clock in our hotel bar we wondered if someone had deliberately turned it forward. It was nearly three in the morning and we were still knocking back the booze. Common sense prevailed and seven very drunk CCS members shambled into the lift and up to the floor our rooms were on. I don't remember my head hitting the pillow that night. I do remember the alarm clock in the room going off at 5:30, two-and-a-half hours later, because I'd had the good sense to set it before I went to the bar.

Jesus, I felt rough. In fact, I didn't even feel rough, I was still bevvied and not just a little bit either. The line I walked between the bed and the shower was anything but straight. I nearly did myself a mischief on the little dressing table. One inch to the right and I wouldn't have been fathering kids. But I knew that if I could just get to the shower, I'd be fine. A shower was my cure-all. Get the head under the water and just stand there and everything would come back into focus. It didn't. If anything I felt worse. I'd had so little sleep and so much booze that nothing was working inside my head.

I practically sleepwalked my way into my clothes. Dressing was simple. The classic 'These Colours Don't Run' T-shirt and the white Hibs away jersey over the top of it. Pair of jeans, trainers, blue baseball cap. Sorted. Except I wasn't sorted. I was like an extra from *The Night of the Living Dead* as I shuffled out of the room, clutching my bruised dangly bits after the earlier collision with the dressing table. I hobbled to the lift and took it down to the ground floor and my spirits were at least slightly raised when I saw the rest of the boys. They'd been as sensible as me and set their alarms. They felt just as rotten as I did.

Everyone was wearing the same white Hibs top; that had been agreed in advance. Another of the boys had done the same as me and donned a blue baseball cap. But all of us were the same colour as our shirts and we were still steaming. If we didn't sober up before we reached the studios they'd never let us appear. We thought about black coffee but at that moment the minibus drew up. The driver took one look at us and offered a friendly, 'All right lads' but the look on his face said it all. He knew we were wrecked. If he hadn't sussed it before we boarded the minibus, it wouldn't have taken Hercule Poirot to work it out. We were still stinking of booze.

It was just a short hop to the studios and we at least found a canteen there where we could grab a bit of breakfast and try and sober up. Then it was off to the studio where the programme would go out live to the nation. We had a quick look about before we were led off to a little room where we were told we could relax before the show. It was boiling in there and one of the boys, Bobby, took off his Hibs shirt to cool down. Just then one of the producers for the show came in and clocked his T-shirt. He looked as though he was about to pass out as he read it. You could almost see the thought running through his mind. He had a bunch of casuals on his show. We knew we had to calm him down and we assured him we would be no bother. We just wanted to put Hibs on the telly. But his bottle had gone. He was in a little room with a bunch of casuals who stank like Tennent's brewery and who were wearing shirts boasting that they were casuals. And he was about to put them on live television. He was very clear in his instructions. Don't make any noise unless you're invited to by the presenters and do not, under any circumstances, allow those T-shirts to be caught on camera. We nodded meekly, desperate to put him at his ease.

Of course, there wasn't a cat in hell's chance of the T-shirts staying covered up during the two-hour run of the show. We just had to promise that they would, or we'd never have made it out of that little room and on to the set. Even though we did promise to be good, the look on the producer's face suggested he was thinking of nailing up our door from the outside and locking us in there until the show had ended.

Next to knock on the door was Tim Lovejoy, one of the co-presenters, and a decent bloke. But he mentioned that the producer was having kittens and asked us, very nicely, to be on our best behaviour. We told him the same as we'd told the producer. We just wanted to put Hibs on the telly and he shook our hands warmly and headed off. The other co-presenter was, and still is, Helen Chamberlain. I'll tell you what: she's a game girl as well. Tim Lovejoy must have warned her that not only were the seven of us casuals, but also that we were still boozed up from the night before. Yet she still came along to see us unescorted and repeated the warning about the T-shirts.

Now, Helen Chamberlain is a massive Torquay fan; she comes from the town itself. It was also well known in football circles that she had a tattoo of the Torquay club crest that was not visible to the common or garden passer-by. It was on her arse. And there was no greater certainty in life than this bunch of drunken Scotsmen asking to see it. The bunch of drunken Scotsmen did. Fair play to her, she didn't bat an eyelid. She hitched up the left-hand side of her skirt and there it was. The blue-and-yellow crest of Torquay FC on her bum cheek. Full credit, we didn't think for one minute she'd do that and she left seven Hibs fans speechless. She told us she'd see us on the set and we were all left sitting looking at each other. Eventually, one of the guys said, 'You realise the boys back home are never going to believe us when we tell them that. Think she'd show us again and let us take a picture?' We told him in no uncertain terms that the chances of Helen Chamberlain flashing her thong at us a second time were non-existent.

It was so hot in the little room that most of us dozed off. I wondered if they had turned the heating up on purpose to try and sweat some of the booze out of us. Whatever their thinking, we were a pretty ripe bunch by the time we took our seats in the designated area of the set. The way the programme works is that the celebrity guests for that week are wheeled out when it's their turn to be interviewed by the presenters. But we were there from the off, sitting in two rows, on the opposite side of the set from Tim Lovejoy and Helen Chamberlain. And when they introduced us, we were to burst into a Hibs song and give it big licks. Tim Lovejoy said, 'And today's fans are from Hibs' and we sprang out of our seats and burst into song. Bobby threw in a wee dance as well, right up to the camera that was filming us. And as soon as he was directly in front if it, up came the Hibs top and 'These Colours Don't Run, Hibs Casuals on Tour' was beamed nationwide.

We were killing ourselves. Our promise to behave hadn't even lasted a minute into the show but by then they were stuck with us. To be fair to Tim Lovejoy and Helen Chamberlain, they were laughing too although they covered their eyes as Bobby's shirt came up. We always wound up Bobby by him calling Scotland's ugliest man. I think the producer probably agreed that day.

By the time the show was over we shook hands with everyone – except the producer, who just shot us a disgusted look – and went off to catch the minibus back to our hotel. We were just going to pick up our bags and head for a pub near the station because we had a train to catch back to Edinburgh. Now we'd been all over *Soccer AM* we knew there would be London crews looking for us.

Bobby had every reason not to want to meet up with Millwall.

It was him who'd been sentenced to three years for mobbing and rioting at The Den. The rest of us had been on that trip as well so we figured a pub near the station was the best idea. We found one and had settled down for an afternoon's boozing when Bobby's mobile rang. It was a journalist from the *News of the World*. It turned out some boy from another mob in Scotland had phoned them to say Bobby was one of Scotland's most violent casuals and it was a disgrace he'd been on the telly that morning, masquerading as a decent fan. What a load of bollocks. He wasn't masquerading as anything. He was there as a Hibs fan and he was, and still is, a Hibs fan. Presumably flashing the shirt had sent this moaner over the edge.

Anyway, the journalist started asking Bobby questions about whether we were planning any trouble while we were in London. England were playing France that day at Wembley and the journalist wanted to know if we were heading there to look for a fight. Bobby said, 'We don't know what to do, we'll see what happens.' It was nonsense but he was just winding the boy up. By the time Bobby took that phone call, we'd had enough booze to top us up again. The only thing we were fighting at that point was sleep. We'd had two hours of it in two days. But Bobby was enjoying himself now, laying it on thick for the journalist. He was reminiscing about the battle against Rangers at Slateford, among other great tales. The rest of us were looking at him and shaking our heads because we knew how this was going to end. He just gave us a wink and carried on with his tales of derring-do.

By the time we got on the train we were done. The booze acted as a sleeping pill and I don't think we spoke more than three words to each other before we were all fast asleep. When we got off the train we made straight for the newsagent's and bought a copy of the *News of the World*.

We turned the first couple of pages and figured they had

realised it wasn't much of a story. Then we got to page eleven and there we were in all our glory. Seven drunken arseholes, bellowing at the top of their voices, dancing and clapping. The headline read 'Fans Telly Star is Violent Hibs Casual'. And the story started:

> A psychotic hard man was among a group of so-called foot-ball fans who tricked their way on to a top TV soccer pro-gramme. The seven were shown larking around on Sky Television's popular *Soccer AM* programme yesterday morning. But, incredibly, their ringleader is a member of Scotland's most notorious hooligan gang, the Hibs Casuals – or Capital City Service (CCS). Hardman Bobby Lipscombe was even filmed flashing a T-shirt with the gang's slogan – These Colours Don't Run – printed on a green Union Jack background.

Bobby was delighted to be called a psychotic hard man. The story also called him a tattooed terror further down. He was grinning from ear to ear. We all were. Not only had we had a top weekend, but also the newspapers had preserved it for posterity. We had the picture of ourselves on *Soccer AM*, we'd put the CCS back in the spotlight and we were on a high as we walked out of Waverley station.

If only we could have got Helen Chamberlain's arse into the paper, the weekend would have been damn-near perfect.

21

YOU DON'T TAKE LIBERTIES

My regular resolutions to finally turn my back on the CCS usually lasted as long as it took one of my mates to give me a call. When I came back from Holland for good I was soon hanging around with the boys again, the nice life in Eindhoven now a distant memory. Quite clearly I needed something to shake me out of the constant cycle of fights and arrests and it finally came on 25 January 2003. It was the day that proved to me beyond all doubt there were some crews you would always respect and some crews you would never respect. It was also the day that finished me with life as a casual.

Hibs had to travel to Tannadice to play a Scottish Cup tie against Dundee United and we'd contacted Dundee's mob, the Utility Crew, to check that they were up for a battle before, or after, the match. They sounded positive, so it was game on. The agreement was that we'd call them once we got to Dundee, arrange to meet and get it on providing the coppers didn't stick their oar in. We made sure we were up in Dundee nice and early and, surprise, surprise, there was no great police presence at the station when we arrived.

We had a decent mob with us and we went to a pub called Sinatra's and settled down to have a pint. I called the Utility's top boy and told him where we were. He said, 'We're not going to meet you today. We're not coming out for this one.' I couldn't believe it. It was tough enough to get a battle going in those days because the coppers were all over the top of us. Closed-circuit television was making our lives a misery as well because the old trick of everyone sticking to the same story, and forcing the cops to pick holes in it, were long gone. Now they had film as evidence and the quality was good. They could identify individuals from the tapes and you had no defence; you were bang to rights.

But the area around Tannadice and Dens Park was perfect for a battle because it was a rabbit warren of streets. Yet Dundee, on their own patch, were sitting in some boozer, too scared to come out. It stank. I gave the Dundee boy an earful down the phone and told the boys. They were raging.

But our luck soon turned when I got a call from Rangers. Their crew were also in town because they were on their way to a cup-tie at Arbroath, and they had to change trains in Dundee. They had time to spare and they wanted to meet for a battle before they moved on. We arranged to meet them at the station and the boys were well up for it. Fights with Rangers were always good, even if they were usually tooled up.

We left Sinatra's and headed to the prearranged spot and, true to their word, Rangers were mob-handed. So were we and there was no preamble. After all, Rangers had a train to catch. The two mobs charged at each other and it was the usual Hibs versus Rangers fight, everyone laying it on the line. I was battering into a Rangers boy when I felt a thud on the back of my head and then I heard the sound of glass hitting the tarmac.

Bastard! I'd been bottled on the back of the head.

Then it happened again and I was seriously pissed off at that. My head was badly cut and there was blood trickling down my scalp and ruining my good jacket. But I waded back into the fray and landed some decent blows before the sound of sirens in the distance meant the fight was over. The coppers were on their way and none of us wanted to get nicked so we all scattered.

We still had loads of time to kill before the game so I went to a chemist and bought a big bandage and wrapped it round the cut area of my head. I was wearing a baseball cap anyway so I hoped it wouldn't show too much. Some chance. It was so visible under the cap that when we finally wandered up to Tannadice to pay our way into the ground the cops took one look at me and knocked me back. They wouldn't even let me into the ground. I tried pleading my case but they told me that if I didn't move along they'd nick me so that was that. I told the rest of the boys to go in and watch the game but one of our guys said he'd give it a miss and keep me company while the rest of them went in. He was a good man. The two of us wandered off to find a pub, swearing Dundee had to be the shithole of the world. They had a mob who wouldn't fight, they had coppers who wouldn't let you into the game, what a crap place to have football teams.

As we grumbled and mumbled our way along the street we spotted the Ambassador pub and figured that it looked like the best place to spend the next ninety minutes while Hibs, we hoped, were thrashing United. The two of us walked through the door, strolled up to the bar and ordered two pints of lager. The barman hadn't even picked up the first glass to start pouring the pints before the guy standing next to me at the bar turned around and pushed his face close to mine. 'What team are you two, then?' he asked, full of himself. 'Hibs,' I replied. And the whole pub stood up. Oh shit. They'd done their best to avoid us when we were mob-handed. And now there were only two of us we'd walked straight into their boozer and given them a late Christmas present.

Let me tell you now that if this had been Edinburgh, and two

Utility boys had walked into a pub that was wall-to-wall CCS, we wouldn't have touched them. A mob of fifty against two guys is taking a liberty. But we were under no illusions; CCS rules just didn't apply in Dundee. This became even clearer when two boys got up and barred the exit. They didn't need to draw a picture. This was a bad, bad situation and it was about to get worse.

I decked the boy next to me, my mate did the same, and we made a bolt for the door. We were punching, booting and scrapping our way through bodies and them having such a huge numerical advantage really didn't do them any great favours. Instead of standing back and taking us apart they were all desperate to say they'd done Hibs, and they were getting in each other's way. We somehow managed to battle our way out of the door, after taking a beating, and staggered out into the street.

But the Utility still had the blood lust and they hadn't finished with us yet. We tore off down the street with their mob in hot pursuit. My mate looked back to see if they were gaining on us and ran straight into a pole. He went down like a sack of spuds and he was badly dazed. They were on him in an instant and I had to go back and help him. We weren't going to have another Raymie Morrell on our hands. I waded into the mob but it was hopeless. I was soon down on the ground beside my mate as they laid into us and in that situation all you can do is cover up.

Thankfully, the police were on the scene pretty quickly but we'd had a right kicking. The Utility mob ran as soon as the police arrived and we dragged ourselves off the ground, dusted ourselves down and looked at each other. It could have been worse, much, much worse. Since we'd been denied our pint in the Ambassador we decided to find another pub. We headed down towards Dens Park and found a wee boozer there but we were more careful this time. When we opened the door we checked all around first in case there was a lurking mob. There wasn't, so we might actually get to enjoy a pint here without having to run for our lives.

I suppose most folk would have put what happened down to a bad day at the office but that's not the way it worked with us. There had to be payback because the Utility had taken a liberty. I got on the phone to the boys at the game and told them they had to leave and come and meet us because we'd just had a kicking from fifty Utility. They couldn't believe it. They couldn't believe their mob would be such cowards. We told them which pub we were in and within ten minutes the boys were all there. They were raging and they were desperate for revenge. I phoned the Utility's top boy again and told him we were gunning for them. 'Got your mob with you now, have you', he said. 'We're not interested. We've had our fun for today.' I was so angry I felt like chucking the bloody phone through the window. But we weren't going to let it lie. If they wouldn't come to us, we'd just have to go to them.

We left the boozer five minutes before the game was due to end because we knew the Utility wouldn't hang around until full time if they knew we were after them. We decided to head from Dens Park down into the centre of Dundee and as we made our way through Hilltown I spotted one of the wee bastards who had been in the pub when we got the hiding. I shot across the road to try and grab him and find out where the rest of his mob were hiding. He denied being one of the Utility and claimed he was an Arbroath casual. There was no such thing. But before I could smack him he wriggled out my grasp and ran for his life. That didn't do much to improve my mood.

But as we reached the centre of Dundee we cut up behind the Wellgate Centre towards Sinatra's, the pub we'd started off in. The Utility were in there, having a right good time. They weren't laughing when they saw us standing at the door, calling them outside for a proper fight. They came out and we tore into them. I only ever felt anger fighting against Aberdeen, because of what had happened in the past. The battle was always more of an adrenaline rush for me but there was a rage inside me that day. We were pounding them, giving them a doing, but the coppers arrived too quickly for us to really return the battering they'd given me and my mate. I suppose you can't have it both ways. I was delighted when the cops had turned up quickly earlier in the day. I couldn't be too churlish they turned up quickly again.

The Utility got off their marks again when the police arrived and we walked around the corner and headed back up the street. We'd taken about three paces when two officers jumped out and grabbed me and told me I was being arrested. The policeman and policewoman took me to the station and there were seven or eight other boys from our mob there as well. They had closed-circuit television footage from the battle with Rangers at the train station earlier in the day and they said they were going to study it. If were caught on film we were done. If they couldn't see us we were free to go.

The policeman went away to check the film and he came back and told his colleague he couldn't spot me on the tape. Magic, I thought. I'm getting away with this one. Then the policewoman insisted she would take a look at the tape as well before they released me. And she came back and said, 'Blue baseball cap, blue jacket, you're on the tape.' That was all I needed, an eagle-eyed copper. So I was charged and the policeman said to me, 'Just admit it and you'll be out of here tonight.' There was no chance of that. I wasn't admitting anything. Until the sheriff banged his little hammer and pronounced me guilty I was admitting nothing.

So that was me, banged up in the cells at the police station with some of the other boys. We were kept in until Monday morning, taken to court and bailed to appear at a later date. There was bad news in court. We were being charged with mobbing and rioting.

There was a pub right round the corner from the court and we nipped in for a pint before we caught a train back to Edinburgh. While we were sitting there two of the Dundee boys came in. I was all for battering them there and then because I was still raging with them but the other boys talked me out of it.

I said to them, 'For what you cowards did to me and my mate at the weekend, I should smack you in the face right now.' They had the gall to say, 'That's bit much, is it not.' I said, 'Fifty of you chased two of us out a pub and then gave us a right good kicking. But I'll tell you, I'm not going to smack you, I'm going to tell anyone who is prepared to listen to me just how shite your mob really is.' I hope I've just done that.

Let me put the Dundee mob in context for you. Hibs played Leeds on 31 July 2004 in a pre-season friendly at Easter Road. I'd given it up by then because I had been given a banning order. But the boys still stuck to the same code we'd always followed. You don't take liberties. They met a couple of the Leeds boys at Waverley station and took them to the site they'd chosen for the battle the following day. Leeds were to go to the Hop Step and Jump pub behind Meadowbank stadium. Hibs would go to the Loch Inn, which is on the same street. It would have been perfect for a battle because there were no cameras on that street, so they wouldn't have been disturbed by coppers as they set about each other.

For reasons best known to themselves, Leeds didn't show. They hooked up with Hearts instead and they all went to the Standing Order pub on George Street, presumably because they thought they could ambush Hibs. But after the game it really caught light. There were battles everywhere. Four or five Leeds boys were taken to hospital after getting a doing at Waverley Market, there were battles in the station and on Princes Street and it was madness. The Leeds mob got split and one of their most experienced boys wandered into a pub and found himself surrounded by Hibs boys. It was exactly the same as had happened to us in Dundee. He later admitted he was bricking himself because everywhere he looked there were people who wanted to kill him.

At the same time, down in Waverley station, one of the Hibs boys went to the toilet and was followed in by three Leeds guys who planned on giving him a kicking. The Hibs boy simply pulled out his mobile phone and told them about the tight spot their fella was in up in our boozer. They backed off. And the Leeds boy in the pub didn't get touched, because it would have been taking a liberty to have a whole mob attack one guy. Hibs still gave Leeds a doing that day.

But they didn't cross the line Dundee did.

22

THE BOY BECOMES A MAN

By the end of season 2002/03 I was at a pretty low ebb. I had the mobbing-and-rioting charge from the battle in Dundee hanging over my head and the fallout from that fight had already screwed up my life. The authorities had placed an eighteen-month banning order on me, preventing me from going to any football ground. A condition of that banning order was that I had to sign in at the local police station every Saturday.

Maybe it was the fact that I could no longer go to watch Hibs that was weighing me down. My disillusionment with the casual scene had been growing for some time and now it was enveloping me like a shroud. I was just totally pissed off with life at that point. At the ripe old age of thirty-six, I couldn't even go and watch my local team any more.

But it's funny how life can kick you in the nuts one minute then pick you up by the scruff of the neck the next. One of the first days of the new season, 2003/04, was, of all things, a derby. Cue black cloud of depression. I couldn't go because I was banned from Easter Road. Even if the Hearts mob had grabbed their courage in both hands and actually shown up for a change, I certainly wasn't going battling, not with the mobbing-and-rioting court case looming. And I couldn't even go and see the boys before the game because I had to sign in at the cop shop.

But every inky black cloud has a silver lining. Hibs won the match (which was played on 17 August 2003) 1–0, with Garry O'Connor scoring in the last minute to leave the Hearts fans sick at the outcome and a certain Hibee even sicker because he hadn't been there. Even when you meet up with the boys after that, it's tough to be a part of it because they're talking about a game you didn't even see. They're full of what happened at the game and discussing baiting Hearts fans and all the rest of it and you're almost an outsider. It's a world you don't inhabit for that three or four hours on a Saturday any more.

And what stories are you going to offer them in return? How you put a bit of excitement into your life by signing your name left-handed at the cop shop for a change? But because it had been a derby victory we all arranged to have a right good night out and I couldn't be a wet blanket. I wasn't going to be a miserable sod and spoil the whole night for everyone so I got the good gear on and headed out to Rose Street.

For anyone who doesn't know Edinburgh, Rose Street is a drinker's dream. It's got wall-to-wall pubs and caters for every taste and age of drinker. It was where we normally started and finished our day when we were with the mob. And you know what? Despite my black mood I was having a right good time with the boys. The drink was flowing, the stories were getting taller by the second and I was feeling more relaxed than I had been in weeks. I looked around at the guys and thought I'd been wrong to doubt my commitment to them.

At that moment I felt as though the lot of us would always be together as a mob come hell or high water. I'd no sooner had that thought than I looked across the bar and a face caught my eye. It was one of those moments when you do a double take, because it's someone you think you recognise but you don't want to wave and make an arse of yourself until you're absolutely sure.

Oh, but I knew her all right. It was Donna and she had been my girlfriend way back at the start of secondary school. I don't want to get all Romeo and Juliet about it but it was one of those doomed romances. When I was thirteen I'd been invited to a party by a mate from school and there was a bunch of girls there, Donna being one of them. From what I recall, and she'll kill me for saying this, she told me in no uncertain terms, 'You're going out with me from now on.' Basically, she claimed me. Hey, it was fine by me. She was a lovely-looking girl so I was happy enough she wanted to go out with me.

But there were problems. She went to Broughton High School, I went to Trinity Academy. Her school was full of Hearts fans, I was a Hibee. So every time I went to meet her after school, I was running the gauntlet. It was my first real experience of football battles because I was scrapping with Hearts most days after school just to see my girlfriend. In the end, Donna started skipping school and hanging out with me at my school instead. That was a bad move. You never think of these things at the time because you're young and daft, but parents inevitably find out when you pull a stroke like that. They normally find out because they have a phone and the school has a phone and one calls the other.

We'd been going out together for eighteen months when Donna's parents finally found out. And when they did they went ballistic at the thought of her chucking away her chance of a decent education on a boy, especially when she was barely into secondary school. You can see their point. I'd have thought the same thing. So they grounded her. Fair enough you might think. That would teach us both a bit about patience. But they grounded her for eighteen months, the same amount of time we'd been going out together. She wasn't allowed out to see me in that time so it was no surprise when things ended between us.

But now, there she was, waving back at me from across the bar. I wandered over and we got chatting and caught up on twenty lost years. It turned out she'd been married but her marriage had broken up. She had two kids, Owen and Zoe, and she was completely devoted to them. And, no, she wasn't seeing anyone. It just got better and better.

I gave her my potted history, missing out everything about the Capital City Service. It didn't seem the right time to tell her the young lad she'd been banned from seeing all those years had spent most of the intervening years running riot at football matches around Scotland and Europe. I figured that might scare her off. So I invited her to join us when we moved on to a nightclub. A few of the guys were planning on extending the night out by a few hours by going on to a club and I invited Donna along. To my delight she said yes and a day that had started so badly for me was getting better by the second. You know, as we left the club that night, it seemed as though we'd never been apart. We exchanged phone numbers and I promised to give her a call and see where we went from there. Where we went from there was that we arranged a date, then another date, and another, until we were an item again.

Whenever we were out together, we'd inevitably bump into one of my mates, who was either past or present CCS. Now Donna's not stupid and she sussed out early on from the conversations she heard us having that I was heavily involved with the whole casual thing. When the time came for us to get everything out in the open that was exactly what we did and it had to be done. I'd grown so close to both Donna and her kids that there could be no secrets. I told her everything that had gone on and held my breath, expecting to be shown the door. Instead, she explained quite calmly and rationally that my choice was simple. If I wanted to remain a part of her life, and Owen's and Zoe's, I had to stop running with the CCS. There was no problem with meeting them for a beer or whatever.

But the fighting days were over.

She told me straight that she couldn't have the police coming to the door every other day over some football battle when she had two kids in the house and a good job to hold down. And she was right. It was time to grow up. I'd been running about like a daft laddie since I was eighteen and I had other responsibilities. I had the love of my life and two kids I loved to bits to look after and they didn't need me getting nicked every other weekend. You can't be bringing up kids then disappearing for two days at a time every weekend because you're locked up in some police cell, or worse.

It was different before, I had no one to answer to but myself. If I got nicked nobody was sitting up waiting for me. I was answerable only to me. And with all due respect to any girls I'd gone out with during that period, they weren't girls I'd have wanted to settle down with. Now it was different. I had people I really cared about and who cared about me. Donna was right. The choice was a simple one and it took me seconds to make it.

That was it, my battling days were over.

But there was one very dark cloud on the horizon. I still had the mobbing-and-rioting charge to face. And when the court papers came through I spoke to my lawyer and he warned me I could be looking at eighteen months inside. My heart hit my boots. How the hell could I tell Donna I might be banged up for eighteen months? She'd tell me to sling my hook for sure.

When I got in that night and sat her down and told her what

the lawyer had said her only concern was what we were going to tell Owen. Zoe wasn't a problem at that stage because she was too young to understand what could happen. But I'd forged a real bond with Owen and we knew it would crush him if I suddenly disappeared for a year and a half. She wasn't slinging me out. She was planning how to solve this problem without it breaking us as a family.

In the end, we decided to tell him that I might have to go back to Holland to work again, as I'd done in 2000. I'll tell you, I've told some whoppers in my time. I've lied to coppers, doctors, nurses and lawyers without batting an eyelid. But the hardest thing I've ever done is look into the earnest little eyes of an eight-year-old boy and lie to him. We sat Owen down and explained things just as we'd planned but I felt like a real louse doing it. I felt rotten about it for days and I'm sure Donna did as well. That was when it really hit me that every one of my actions from then on would have consequences I couldn't even begin to imagine. And I had no intention of lying to Owen or Zoe ever again.

By the time I got the train up to Dundee for the court case I was shiting myself. The prospect of doing eighteen months was hardly appealing in itself. The thought of what it would cost me in terms of Donna, Zoe and Owen was way too much to bear. When I was led into the dock, I realised the guy who'd been alongside me on that night in Dundee – and who had also been caught on camera – wasn't there because his charges had been dropped. At that point I feared the worst. It was clear I was being seen as the ringleader and I was certain I was going down.

I pleaded guilty, the lot of us did, and I sat with my head down and my stomach churning, waiting to hear my sentence. When the sheriff sentenced me to a fine of £1,500, I could have leapt that dock and kissed his feet. Sure, it was a lot of money, and it was cash that

I could have spent on the kids, but at least I was free to go back home to my family.

Back home to my family. Even now I love the sound of that.

And once my banning order was over I started taking Owen with me to the game on a Saturday. We're both now season-ticket holders at Easter Road and I coach kids football three nights a week. Owen wants to be a goalkeeper, so I took the SFA coaching course on goalkeeping so I can help him achieve his dream.

I suppose life has come full circle. In years gone by I taught kids the ins and outs of fighting when we coached the Baby Crew. Now I'm teaching the kids how to live a different sort of dream. Zoe's a little princess and if she ever starts dodging school to see a boy we'll ground her for eighteen months. Just joking. Oh, and we've another addition. Carly celebrated her second birthday last Christmas Eve. We all go on family holidays together and have a magic time. I took Owen over to Ireland for Hibs' pre-season games last summer and it was brilliant.

Don't get me wrong: at the time I was running with the CCS I was having a whale of a time. It was great fun for me and I loved the mob like brothers. What we achieved will never be forgotten either. We became Scotland's top mob. But the life I lead now? It's like another world. The only fighting I'd get involved in now would be a fight to protect my family.

Thanks to Donna, the boy finally became a man.

EPILOGUE

On 15 October 2006, Hibs and Hearts played out a 2–2 draw at Easter Road. Following the match, running battles were fought in the city's Lothian Road and Fountainbridge areas. One pub was attacked and several fans drinking inside it were injured. Battles raged in the street outside.

Police set up a special task force to track down the casuals they believed had been involved in the violence. Worried local councillors demanded action and the new task force spent hundreds of hours poring over footage from closed-circuit television in a bid to identify the culprits.

Police were forced to admit it appeared older casuals and younger casuals had joined forces in the bloody battle. They warned the guilty men to turn themselves in while they had the chance. The alternative was an early-morning knock on the door. In a series of dawn raids over the next two months, police arrested a total of forty-two people, ranging in age from their teens to their late thirties.

Derek Dykes was not one of them.